T5-BQB-630

Faked Disability: A Shame of America

An Insult to the Medical Profession, A Disgrace to the Legal Profession

by

Joseph H. Miller, M.D.

Rear Admiral Joseph H. Miller

Bloomington, IN   Milton Keynes, UK

authorHOUSE®

AuthorHouse™
1663 Liberty Drive, Suite 200
Bloomington, IN 47403
www.authorhouse.com
Phone: 1-800-839-8640

AuthorHouse™ UK Ltd.
500 Avebury Boulevard
Central Milton Keynes, MK9 2BE
www.authorhouse.co.uk
Phone: 08001974150

© *2007 Joseph H. Miller, M.D.. All rights reserved.*

No part of this book may be reproduced, stored in a retrieval system, or transmitted by any means without the written permission of the author.

First published by AuthorHouse 7/18/2007

ISBN: 978-1-4343-0403-2 (sc)
ISBN: 978-1-4343-0404-9 (hc)

Library of Congress Control Number: 2007903510

Printed in the United States of America
Bloomington, Indiana

This book is printed on acid-free paper.

Acknowledgments

To Common Sense Which is Not Common

I would like to give special appreciation to people who have heard me speak on this subject and have consistently asked me to write this book. I have discussed this book with many people. Every one of them is aware of faked disability in this country and is disgusted by it.

Dedication

This book is dedicated to the greatest Christian parents who were wonderful, humble, hard working, loving, trusting, self-sacrificing, and non-judging in all things.

Joe H. Miller, Sr. D.D.
Leta Elsie Caddell
And
Charles Cleveland Parker
Letha Earnestine Parker

Table of Contents

Preface

"More that 40 million people in the United States consider themselves to have a physical or mental impairment that significantly affects life's activities."

"Impairment ratings attempt to link objective measures of organ function with the functional tasks of performing activities of daily living. Thus, impairment ratings do not reflect an individual's ability to work. The complexity of these determinations as well as limitations in resources and in the level of existing medical and scientific knowledge made this impossible. The scientific evidence is too limited. Changes in legal interpretations of disability are needed. The current compensation system provides incentives for decreased function." Finally, in the referenced article it admits that time, personnel and funds are needed so patients with impairments can be "fairly compensated." It does not mention how one approaches the patient who is trying to defraud the system. My review of the disability system in this country suggests that there is no one in control. (28)

This report approaches the low back pain problem from a scientific point of view. If the injury is not consistent with long term persistent symptoms, an adequate back exam reveals no objective physical abnormalities, the latest diagnostic tests do not reveal pathology consistent with the symptoms, and multiple non-organic finding are present, the patient must be declared "fit for duty" (Work). This fits all the criteria for "beyond all reasonable doubt" however, in the rare case that a correct diagnosis is not made, it will always show itself at a later date. I can relate cases where this happened. The diagnosis was always something unrelated to an injury and was an incidental disease process.

I received a call from a very well known and prestigious medical institution concerning my cousin. He was one of the toughest, most honest, most capable athletes, and was as hard a working individual as I have ever known. The physician after his introduction of his credentials and naming the institution informed me that my cousin needed a psychiatrist. He stated that all my cousin's studies had been negative for his diffuse complaints. I could tell that he had made a fixed diagnosis and had ceased to think. He was somewhat taken back by my spontaneous answer. I said, "You need to go back and study him further, I can tell you he does not need a psychiatrist." A week later a diffuse malignant process in the bone marrow was discovered. My cousin was dead in six weeks. He died of a disease process unrelated to work or injury.

A Plea for the Renewal of America

All Americans must become aware of the problem of the abuse of the disability system and become active in the elimination of those who are cheating the system.

It will not be solved unless Americans want it to be and eliminate the abuse! "Eliminate laziness as it breeds, the mental alertness to avoid hard work." (25, p. 323)

The famous **Hippocrates:**
"Life is short, art is long, the opportunity fleeting, experiment treacherous, judgment difficult." (6, p. 73)

Work for the male is a natural activity. God put Adam in the Garden of Eden and told him to work it. (Genesis 2:15) This was before man sinned when the devil enticed Eve to eat of the "tree of knowledge" and she enticed Adam to do the same. Apparently man's destiny was to spend all his days working in the garden. To "dust thou art, and unto dust thou shalt return." (Genesis 3:19) This does not say that man's mortality is the result of disobedience. He was made from dust as a mortal creature who with time would return to dust. As a spirit or soul we were known before we were born and are as a soul eternal (Jeremiah 1:5; Isaiah 49:1), but our bodies were created to be mortal.

Attention all Americans. We are slowly being destroyed by people who do not work. The politicians in both parties cannot act because it would cause a loss of votes and thus the loss of their jobs. Robert J. Samuelson in his article notes that in 1956 the federal budget spent 60% on national defense and 22% on payments to individuals who were not working. In 2006 amazingly the figures are reversed with 20% being spent on national defense and 60% on payments to non-working individuals. We are an infected welfare country. (Newsweek, 19 February 2007, p. 39) **We must wake up!**

Prologue

Hippocrates (460-377 B.C.) said, "The physician must not only be prepared to do what is right himself, but also to make the patient cooperate."**(21, p. 54)**

Edmund Burke (1729-1797), "It is not, what a lawyer tells me I may do; but what humanity, reason, and justice, tell me I ought to do." **(6, p. 344)**

Oliver Cromwell (1599-1658) "Necessity hath no law. Feigned (faked) necessities, imaginary necessities are the greatest cozenage (cheat, defraud) that men can put upon the Providence of God, and make pretenses to break known rules." **(6, p. 254)**

Charles Caleb Colton "Judges are the only civil delinquents who must be necessarily chosen among themselves." (Lawyers) **(25, p. 322)**

Epictetus "Man is his own enemy lying in wait for him. He must keep guard and watch on himself." **(42, p. 694)**

Plato "Others may have the power to put me to death, but they do not have the power to harm me." **(42, p. 695)**

C.S. Lewis "Every disability conceals a vocation. If we can only find it and turn the necessity to a glorious gain. **(36 p.304)**

Chapter I.
Introduction

A Warning to America

"You cannot bring prosperity by discouraging thrift; you cannot strengthen the weak by weakening the strong; you cannot help the wage earner by pulling down the wage payer; you cannot help the poor by destroying the rich; you cannot build character and courage by taking away a man's initiative and independence; and you cannot help men permanently by doing for them what they could and should do for themselves." **Abraham Lincoln**

Phaedrus describes his concept of Utopia to Socrates in Plato's *Republic* (1513) **(39, pp. 614-616)**. By putting all sorts of "idle people to profitable occupation including in the same class, priests, women, noblemen, gentlemen, and 'sturdy and valiant beggars' that the labor of all may be reduced to six hours a day." Society becomes strained and inefficient when there are large numbers of people not working for the common good. In the United States three workers are supporting one non-worker.

The psychological effects of malingering can be horrible. It destroys an individual as a person. He has fallen into a trap and has been enslaved by a generous system, which is quite easy to defraud. The mind has shifted to things and there is no room for people, places, or love. There is left only an inner world of pure human content and action.

It is a rare person who under proper conditions will not accept a hand out from the government or big business. There are also people

1

who will starve to death before they will accept charity. It should be made very clear that every American that I know believes in giving all the aid possible to people with **real** disability and even more than is available. This book is not about the honest person who is truly disabled and needs help. My wife and I personally and also our church have provided aid to people who desperately needed it before the government programs could get started. I have provided free medical care to many people in need. All Americans are thankful to be a part of **real** needed charity.

Many people have the mentality of believing that they are entitled to welfare from the big government **if they decide they want it**. Star Parker describes the poor as being divided into three groups including the "economically challenged, the lazy poor, and the poor in spirit." They fall into a "spiritual and economic poverty." **(3)**

The question must be asked, "Is it fair to society and to the patient in particular to provide him with 'eating bread' of idleness when it has been obtained by fraud?" Eating the bread of the Lord's Supper unworthily is a sin against God. Eating the bread of society by lying is sinning against God and society. Doctors and lawyers, are you also sinning against God and society when you knowingly, falsely or ignorantly help a person get undeserved money from the government or big business?

The psychic effect of unintelligent treatment and sick pay often leaves the effects of a perverted mental outlook and a morbid introspection. Even the preparation of legal proceedings, which must produce exaggerations, adds to the destruction of the individual. **(2, p. 255)**

One can assume that in the **majority** of cases with a normal examination and normal objective tests that the alleged pain is mental and not physical.

Sir John Collie in 1917 tells of a man who earned more on disability than he did at working. **(2, p. 261)**

Years ago I had a doctor friend who had a small farm. He loved working there and spent every free weekend and his time off on the farm. He never took a vacation. One Saturday when he arrived at the farm all twenty-one of his employees were sitting on his front porch with this message, "Doctor we have just learned that we can move to Memphis and get on a social program that pays within five dollars of what you pay. It is not worth working for five dollars a week." They left never to be heard from again.

Collie also tells of a patient who had been on crutches for eight years. He bathed in the holy well at the shrine of St. Winifrede. He was cured like being "shot out a gun." He left his crutches at the well and returned to normal activities. (2, p. 259) Before one draws a conclusion note this next case.

I was referred a 29 year old attractive female patient who had undergone five back operations. Her exam was remarkably normal. Her MRI was normal except for the expected postoperative scar tissue. It is rare for any person with five back operations to return to work. She did not need further surgery because her exam did not suggest an acute problem. She asked me what she should do? I was very busy that day and in a spontaneous moment I told her the hard truth. Medicine had nothing else to offer her. I told her that there was nothing structurally wrong with her and that the only person who could help her was herself. I saw her eight years later in a restaurant for the second time. She approached me with this story. She said I made her very mad, and she was going to "show me" how wrong I was. She threw away her pain medicine, discontinued the physical therapy, and returned to her work. She had been working and living a normal life for eight years. Every knowledgeable physician will know that this is very rare for any patient after five back operations.

In the old days the terminology for faked back pain was "railway spine," "hysterical spine", (2, p. 270) or "greenback poultice spine."

Edmund Burke notes, "We must soften into a credulity below the milkiness of infancy to think all men virtuous. We must be tainted with a malignity (malicious behavior) truly diabolical, to believe all the world to be equally wicked and corrupt." **(5, p. 168)**

Samuel Taylor Coleridge quotes from *Tragedies of Shakespeare's Othello* "Iago's Soliloquy, The motive–hunting of motiveless malignity." **(5, p. 233) John Bartlett** adds, "How awful." **(6, p. 402)**

From *The Red Badge of Courage*, "At times he regarded the wounded soldiers in an envious way. He perceived persons with torn bodies to be peculiarly happy. He wished that he, too, had a wound, a red badge of courage." **(7, p. 68)**

Ammianus Marcellinus, famous historian, in his *Books of Deeds* covering 96-378 A.D., at a time when the Roman world was about to collapse relates that, " the bureaucracy consisted of a huge mass of lawyers." **(7, p. 370)** The judges were likewise described as "utterly fraudulent." **(7, p. 376)** The clergy likewise seems to show no effect on the prevention of war or social abuse. On the eve of the French Revolution there were 200,000 clergy in France. 1,700,000 adults were killed which reduced the male population by 16%. **(37, pp. 63, 69)**

Epicurus (341-270 B.C.) founded a school of philosophy, which taught that "pleasure (that is freedom from pain and peace of mind) was the goal of life." **(9, p. 368)** It is important to note that in the ancient philosophy pleasures of the sensual (wine, women, and song) are inferior because they are followed by pain, and "the sensualist's pleasure never achieves total freedom." Real pleasure in ancient times contrasted with sensual pleasure of modern times means, "being neither pained in the body nor troubled in the soul." One who is looking for personal gain has both, "his troubled soul magnifies his pain." (Miller) Pain is not just physical pain, but includes many problems of life such as famines, etc. Life is not at the mercy of fickle fortune or an obsessive individualism. Epicurus renounced and abstained from politics. His famous quote pertinent to our discussion is, "You must free yourself from the prison of politics and the daily round." One cannot achieve happiness by withdrawing from the world, but must live within it as a *useful part not a dependent one*. **(9, p. 371-372)**

The stoics deny that pleasure (no pain, no trouble in the soul) is the best thing. They extend this to include "joy" which is a level above and is the result of a "rational elation." What the mind assents to or dissents from due to its own nature is something within our power. We all have revelations, ideas that come to our minds; they may be good or bad. Revelations based on truth are true. Revelations are false when they are based on untruth. **(9, p. 373, 377, 379)**

Many of the ancients were stoical. (Not affected by passion or feeling, indifferent to pain.) Two physicians, **Herophilus** (270 B.C.) and **Erasistratus** (260 B.C.) developed a diagnostic technique based on different types of pulse, were interested in new drugs, and described and named the duodenum, etc. They were given criminals from the prison by their kings of Egypt. They dissected the criminals alive, while they were still breathing, and observed parts which nature had formerly concealed. They did not think it cruel by causing pain to guilty men to seek remedies for innocent people of every age. **(9, p. 383-384)** This shows an extreme of human mental deviation.

A note about hypochondria which is a mentality centered on imaginary ailments from the 1ˢᵗ edition of *"Medicine"* (1768-1771):

"The hypochondriac passion is a spasmodico-flatulent affliction of the stomach and intestines, arising from an inversion or perversion of their peristaltic motion, and by a consent of parts, throwing the whole nervous system into irregular motions, and disturbing the whole animal economy. The disease is attended with such a train of symptoms, that it is a difficult task to enumerate them all; for there is no function or part of the body, that is not soon or late a sufferer by its tyranny." **(11, p. 7)**

This 250-year-old observation relates that the hypochondriac mind can and does on occasions affect all parts of the body.

This book will only relate to the faked ailments in the low back.

It has been known for at least 61 years that faked illness is an enemy to a country. During World War II, the Germans used shells to scatter hundreds of messages that were labeled, "World War No. 2 is almost over." Printed on both sides were instructions on how to feign (fake) illness. The advice, "Better a few weeks ill than all your life dead." The Germans' message as in Dr. Liddle's paper is quoted, "Nobody can say that as a good soldier you haven't done your duty. But no man in the world will ever blame you for not wishing to be one of its last victims. Toward the end of the war the death rate rises. We will teach you the rules of the game." (How to fake illness.) The Germans gave several principles to faking illness including, "You hate this faked illness. You wish you could still fight; stick to just one kind of disease as too many troubles make a doctor suspicious; and don't tell the doctor too much, you will never be found out if you say too little."

The Germans taught me a lot about techniques of malingering thirty-six years ago when I read the article. I will quote some of the article's instructions to show that **malingering is a science** and a **trained physician** is required to detect it in some cases. Examples of the Germans' recommendations for faking to the American soldier:
- Soak turpentine on a cotton and place in your shoe. Wash it away before being examined.
- Rub gasoline to scarify your skin. Tell the doctor you have no idea what caused it.
- Take a teaspoon of 10% potassium iodide before meals for five days, which causes an iodine skin reaction.
- Create castor oil dysentery, and cut your finger to add blood in your stools.
- Chew and swallow a dozen castor beans. Tell the doctor your stomach hurts.
- Add a little ground up castor beans under the eyelids

overnight.

- Apply a silver nitrate stick to the tonsils.
- Gargle with a yellow mustard or ginger solution just before you see the doctor. Tell the doctor that swallowing is painful.
- Tie rubber tubing around your "funny bone" to create ulnar nerve palsy.
- Take eight or more thyroxine tablets daily until your pulse goes above 100. Tell the doctor you are nervous, irritable and can't sleep and you will be telling the truth.
- Take a supply of dried blood powder daily. Complain of upper abdominal pain. Say it is better with milk. Is it an ulcer?
- Create jaundice by taking digitalis and picric acid orally.
- Smoke many cigarettes, take digitalis, and complain of severe chest pain.
- This last one guarantees a big vacation. Develop a smoker's cough; mix blood from a finger cut, and smegma bacilli from under the prepuce. (Smegma bacilli are identical to the tuberculosis bacteria.) The doctor will tell you to not cough on him and wear a mask on your vacation.

The soldier is assured that none of the above will kill him. (**12, pp. 785, 875.**)

My second active duty with the Navy was in 1953 at a Navy hospital. There were so many appendectomies that the chief of surgery let me perform two of them as a third year medical student. I was told that "Navy" men had visited the library and learned the clinical syndrome of appendicitis. They knew the symptoms better than the doctor who would be on night call in the Emergency Room. The appendix was saved until the night before one was to leave on an undesirable assignment. At which time a visit to the Emergency Room with the knowledge he had learned would guarantee him an operation and cancellation of his assignment.

I had finished my residency in neurosurgery and I thought I had become the "smartest man in the world". I was appointed chief of neurosurgery at the National Naval Medical Center in Bethesda, Maryland. I relieved the senior neurosurgeon in the entire Armed Forces because he liked me. This is noteworthy since I was the junior neurosurgeon in all the Armed Forces. The residents assigned to my service out-ranked me. He told that if we went to war he was going to take me with him. My head swelled even more. Then he said, "I am taking you with me because I want your liquor allowance."

A retired Navy chief came in with a classic syndrome of a ruptured lumbar disk. I did a myelogram on him, which was negative. One day when I was still trying to decide what to do, the Admiral Commanding Officer came to see me. When he reached my office he saw the Navy chief. He ran down the ward and they hugged each other. They had served together many times. When we were back in my office he told me that the chief had had 10-12 myelograms. He went to a Veterans Hospital in the North for the summer and a Veterans Hospital in the South for winter. When he wanted to visit Washington, he came to Bethesda or Walter Reed. At that time his complaint guaranteed a month in the hospital. Some patients show an amazing tolerance to painful procedures and are able to sustain multiple hospitalizations. This is especially true and since the advent of the painless CT and MRI it has become even easier.

To further show my "brilliance" I had a Navy active duty patient who was over his neuro problem, but was overweight. He was smart and a good addition to the Navy. I felt I should help him lose weight. I placed him on a 1000-calorie diet and told him I would not see him again for three weeks. (He was to remain on the hospital ward.) When I did see him he had gained ten pounds. I was shocked. After an investigation I learned that he was not only getting the 1000-calorie diet tray, but he was also receiving a regular tray.

All this reveals that a "smart and self trained" malingerer can virtually always "fool" a smart, but untrained physician.

I have since developed and taught all over the world a technique of detecting a malingerer.

A report in 1970 reveals an added problem concerning the diagnosis of malingering and returning the patient to work. In this case it was Air Traffic Controllers. The question is asked, "Can a malingerer against his will be discharged to go back to work that involves the lives of thousands?" It was obvious that thousands of air traffic controllers were staying home and using "faked" sickness as a negotiation tool.

There was also mention of a long line of politicians, government officials, and racketeers that have used unfavorable medical reports to stall courtroom appearances and congressional hearings and even to stay out of jail. They did not claim their condition was job related. **(13, pp. 15, 16)**

Another question related to me years ago was that of an unmarried military aviator who was obligated for several more years of duty who became pregnant and wanted out of the service. Legally there was an obligation to stay in the service. However, one must ask the question, "Is it smart to force a person to fly a forty million dollar airplane when they do not want to?" (And the baby is at home crying.)

Who does not know of a child who has been kept home from school as being ill because the family wanted to leave early on a vacation? Faked sickness is a way of life in America beginning in childhood.

Sick leave is a blessing and a curse. Just look at the records. Many employees always take all their sick leave each year and others do not take any over a period of many years. Paid sick leave has become an expected benefit. It is very expensive because of those who abuse it.

The air traffic controllers clearly brought to our attention a serious problem. *The doctors disagreed with each other*. A doctor versus doctor battle began. One physician said 50% to 60% of the controllers he examined needed psychiatric care. Another prominent physician doubled that figure. (13, pp. 15, 16) Another physician said it was not a medical issue, but a social one. My review shows that it is a moral issue in both groups. There are hundreds of medically healthy people who have no trouble getting the diagnosis they want. Doctors are motivated by sympathy and money.

"Is he really sick?" This is a dilemma more and more physicians may face as time goes on.

A profound statement made in their report is supported by this author in this report. It is, "If we can tell if a person is sick, we can certainly tell if he is not sick." (13, pp. 15, 16)

Nicholas Gotten, in a famous report (14, pp. 865-868) noted that with "whiplash" injuries in most instances the initial injury seemed "trivial or minor". "Psychoneurotic" symptoms were prevalent and a dominant factor. The symptoms were persistent and there was a lack of a response to treatment. A number of patients refused to carry out the doctor's instructions. Symptoms included profound emotional reactions such as nervousness, instability, insomnia, and sweating of the hands. It was felt that these symptoms were inconsistent with pathological possibilities. These inconsistent symptoms resulted in the following rewards: household help, new air conditioner, new car, new house and a vacation in Florida. They were also, an excuse for avoiding unpleasant tasks and a means of securing recognition from other members of the family, neighbors, friends, and even children.

The significant force of the study revealed that after the legal settlement of claims the vast majority returned to normal work and required no further medical care.

In another report (13, p. 15, 16) it was noted, "In countries with advanced social security mechanisms, notably Britain and West Germany, you have higher illness rates. It is sort of a tax on industry. People get better the day after their benefits run out."

Refusal of medical care (Physical Therapy, exercises, etc.,) is also a sign of malingering. Why take the trouble to go for treatment if you know you don't need it?

Recently a United States Postal Service clerk was convicted by a federal jury of faking impairment to collect disability benefits from worker's compensation and the Veteran's Administration. He collected $406,000 dollars over a ten-year period. During this time he also worked on other jobs. (Tribune Staff Report. *"Jury says man faked disability."* TheTimes-Tribune 18 Feb. 2005. 28 February 2007.<http://www.thetimestribune.com/site/printerFriendly. cfm?brd=2185&dept_id=416046&ne...html>).

(A postal employee told me that back injuries were very common among postal clerks. Many postal clerks have a permit stating that they cannot lift, which adds work for other employees. They told me they have been instructed not to even reach over the counter to pick up a small letter type package.)

In another case a mother and adult son are being prosecuted for faked disability. They received $110,000 over a 10-year period. ("Prosecutors: Video Proves Man Faked Disability." NBC NEWS. com.6December2006.http://www.nbc4.com/news/10476845/detail. html).

There is another report of a "con-artist" faking paraplegia for cash that repeatedly filed claims and lawsuits for noncompliance with the American with Disabilities Act. When they were arrested they jumped from a wheelchair and were quickly caught. There is also pending in this same case two counts of insurance fraud.

A father defrauded his company of over $50,000 in nine months by falsely claiming his son had cancer and he needed to be off from work. A person related to the case said, "It's incredibly hard to understand why somebody would do something like this." (56, p.16) This book tries to answer this question. One must accept that there are people, who are thieves, pathological liars, have no personal morality or ethics, and have voluntarily allowed themselves to be overcome by greed, (In other words they think different than most people.) They are crooks and must be identified as such. When the realities of life are recognized it is not hard to understand. When it is understood as such it must be promptly dealt with, as any other criminal would be.

Chapter II.
The Mendicant Orders:

Mendicant means begging, therefore, Mendicant Orders were begging Orders. They were particularly noted in the middle ages (13th century) and included the Franciscans, Dominicans, Augustinians, and Carmelites. Each group utilized begging as a means to greater ends. It is clear that St. Francis never meant for begging to replace manual labor. The Dominicans are an interesting group. They were the Order of Preachers dedicated to the salvation of souls. As an aid they adopted poverty and begging. (Some modern television preachers are smarter in that they beg, but have not decided on poverty.) A group called the Minors was less rigid and used begging for their own working genius. The Augustinians and Carmelites organized other hermits into begging brotherhoods. This was a useful means to have a religious vocation.

The **Beghards** allowed only male membership and contained other groups such as the French wanderers who begged and were known as beggars. They were condemned as heretics and died out in the 14th century.

The **Dervish** (A Persian word for begging) was an Islamic self-denial order. They were known for their devotional exercises, which included repetitious chants with bodily motions. They sometimes went into a trance and many included self-laceration.

The **faker or Faqir** (Arabic for poor) was a Moslem monk of self-denial who was a wandering beggar and even known as a miracle-worker. They later separated from the Moslems and became an independent order.

Monasticism was a concept used to devote life living in seclusion from the world. (I had a secretary years ago who claimed to be a member of the Order of Man. She said, "Our purpose is to bring men back into the world." I never understood what she meant by that. She was a good secretary who later disappeared without even picking up her last paycheck.) Monastic groups have been noted in every religion and are pre-Christian.

They have included two groups of Jews, the Essenes (allowed men only) and the Therapeutic. (Philo of Alexandria described the Therapeutic in an essay concerning the Contemplative Life. They included men and women. They were self-denying and pious and hoped to obtain perfection. They only gathered together on the Sabbath, which was every fiftieth day and included an all night festival. (**15, p. 784**) The Christian monasticism began in Egypt in the 3rd century. They were more like hermits. They apparently felt the need to work. Since **work seemed to violate their code of life**, they developed the concept that their work was "to be done for its own sake and was not a mere occupation" and thus did not bring them back into the world. All this did not work out so by the 13th century they all merged into great begging orders.

The last group that I have been able to identify includes the **Trinitarians** or **Order of the Holy Trinity**. They were founded in 1198 during the Crusades. Their purpose was to obtain the release of the Christian captives from the infidels. By the 17th Century they became "begging" friars and continued to make social contributions.

The begging friars (**16, p. 1070**) aroused much hostility among the bishops, the secular clergy, and the universities. William of St. Amour led the opposition. St. Thomas Aquinas and St. Bonaventure wrote in their defense. In 1256 Alexander IV ruled in their favor. The

National Conference of Bishops in 1953 determined the norms on begging, and this was binding even in the mendicants (Beggars).

The Trinitarians (17, p. 427) sometimes offered themselves as substitutes for the Moslem Christian captives.

St. Francis became a traveling preacher living in poverty and begging.

The Brothers Minor or Grey Friars, the Preachers or Black Friars, the white Friars, and the Austin Friars were some of the names of the begging groups.

The **Dominicans** and **Franciscans** attached themselves to the universities and by their dedication to the religious life devoted themselves to theology. It is said they brought scholastic theology to its apex in the 13th and 14th centuries. (It's been downhill ever since.)

There was a conflict in the Order of Preachers between those who desired a stern order of life and those who would ease it. The stern order won in 1517 when the Pope declared them to be the true Order of St. Francis. When Martin Luther suddenly decided to become a monk he entered one of their houses. In southern Italy a stern group known as Mincins was formed.

Thucydides said, "Whatever be the obscurity or poverty condition of a man he can still benefit his country. To avow poverty with us is no disgrace; the true disgrace is in doing nothing to avoid it. Man does not neglect his country because he is taking care of his own household. A man who does is not considered harmless, but useless." **(42, pp. 758-59)**

A letter to Congress **(18, p. 19)** signed by The American Baptist Churches USA, the Evangelical Lutheran Church in America, Presbyterian Church (USA), the Jewish Council for Public Affairs, Friends Committee on National Legislation, the National Council of Churches and NET-WORK, a national Catholic social justice lobby, and others urged Congress to reauthorize the 1996 welfare law for five years. This amazing statement is included, "Long-term reauthorization is needed to strengthen the program so families can move out of poverty." This makes these people slaves to the United States Government and plants in them a personal sense of uselessness. Getting people out of poverty by **Charity** does not strengthen our nation. (These are the modern government supported mendicant orders.)

Epictetus said, "Let him who wished to be free not wish for anything that depends on others or else he is bound to be a slave." **(42, p. 685)**

Slavery is returning to this country in a different form. It is more mental than physical.

Joseph Brown, quotes, "Too many recipients of charity do their best to make us cynical about our giving." He quotes a person who works for a charity, "Over the years I have noticed a dramatic increase in the entitlement mentality of the clients we serve and many of those we serve by the charity go back to the same dysfunctional lifestyle that put them on our doorstep to begin with." He continues, "Some, including some government agencies, are not getting the most for their contributions Many of our clients have expensive computers, digital cameras, cell phones, and of course everyone can continue to smoke, yet they are asking us for shelter, food, and money for gas and laundry." This clearly shows that America's poorly controlled generosity is producing an increasingly degenerate and fraudulent society. The number one story is that of the church in Memphis that gave a new house to a couple from New Orleans after Hurricane Katrina. Without ever moving into the house they sold it for a profit, laughed (about the "suckers") and moved back to New Orleans. **(38, p. 1)**

Aristotle said, "When man deviates from normal conduct it leads to vice or absurdity." **(42, p. 823)**

C.S Lewis was asked the question, "What is duty?" His answer, "Well. I suppose work." **(36, p. 169)**

Begging is noted in every country in the world. It has recently been reported that a beggar can earn seven times as much in Cuba as a worker. Medicaid fraud by "involving doctors, nursing homes, pharmacies, medical equipment companies, etc. has increased 75% over the previous year. (2005). **(22, p. 7)**

Begging is a massive business in this country. No one knows the extent in numbers. Some are homeless and some are not. There are so many beggars that many consider them dangerous since they locate at Interstate exits and other highway busy intersections. A recent report reveals a classic case of a thirty seven year old on Social Security disability checks for twenty years. He holds a sign saying he cannot work regularly. If he can work part time and chase cars on the expressway exits, one needs to hear a diagnosis. (I cannot think of one that fits his case. If he can work, he can work.) It is obvious why he does not work when he can make seventy-five dollars a day begging. That is another blight on America.

When one learns there is *"Thieves in the Temple,"* the situation seems almost so widespread that it may be hopeless. It has recently been discovered that in 85% of Roman Catholic dioceses there has been embezzlement of church money. In 11% more than $500,000 was stolen. **(29)** In one year there were seventy-five banks robbed within fifty miles of Atlanta. This makes Jesse James a sissy.

Those begging and faking disability have been obscure social and immoral parasites and must be revealed by society, government, and by good science that detects them as such.

Begging, bragging, and stealing all seem to go together; **many times "titles" violate the Christian principle of self-denial.** This is in my opinion noted in the following: "I am a Franciscan, I am a Dominican, I am an Augustinian, I am a Carmelite, I am an Order of Preachers, I am an Order of Minors, I am a Beghard, I am a Dervish,

I am a Faqir, I am a Monk, I am a Pharisee, I am a Sadducee, I am an Essene, I am a member of the Order of the Holy Trinity, I am a member of Brothers Minor, Grey Friars, the Preachers, Black Friars, White Friars, and Austin Friars to name a few."

Cyprian (date of birth unknown, converted 19 April 246 A.D. and martyred 14 September 258 A.D.) describes one of the most interesting groups in history. (He describes a group called the "Brides of Christ" who had no organization. The earliest formation of their societies was to "meet the needs of homeless virgins". They had not taken a vow and were in a state of limbo (uncertainty). Cyprian ranked the Virgins next to the Martyrs. Some of the virgins were obviously women of influence. Notice how they dressed in 250 A.D. "They buried the neck in masses of gold chains and pearls, piled their hair in grape –like clusters, loaded the arms and feet with bracelets, outlined the almond-like eye with antimony (a silvery white metallic chemical) dyed the cheeks with crimson falsehood, and tipped the toes and fingers with henna (a reddish brown dye). Cyprian does not say how they were supported. However those not given in marriage were the "equality of angels." **(43, pp. 52-57)**

Today it is, "I am a Calvinist, I am a Baptist, I am a Methodist, I am a Catholic, etc." sometimes we insult God by saying, " I am a Christian Calvinist, I am a Christian Baptist, I am a Christian Pentecostal, etc." The report that *"I am a Christian"* is getting more unusual. An experienced soul winner will repeatedly report that when the question, "Are you a Christian?" is asked, the answer is frequently, "I am a member of such and such church."

If you are an unashamed "born again" (new person) Christian and are asked, "Are you a Christian?" Say, "Yes." Any other answer makes you suspect. This statement might be even better, "Yes, I am a Christian," Are you?"

In London a young preacher handed me a tract. I stopped in front of him to look at it. He said, "Are you a Christian?" I said, "Yes, are you?" He weakly said, "Ha, Ha". I said, "Why are you passing out tracts?" He replied, "I want people to know about 'our' religion." Then I asked, "Whose religion is that?" He looked at me and said, "Jesus." I said, "Very good" and walked on. Communication, Communication, is vital for us!

Chapter III.
Religious Quotes

Galatians 6:4 "But let every man prove his own work, and then shall he have rejoicing in himself alone, and not in another."

A.   Bible Quotes and Feigning (faking)

I Samuel 21:13 (King James Version)
"And he changed his behaviour before them, and feigned himself mad in their hands, and scrabbled on the doors of the gate, and let his spittle fall down upon his beard."

I Samuel 21:13 (New International Version)
"So he pretended to be insane in their presence; and while he was in their hands he acted like a mad man. Making marks on the doors of the gate and letting saliva run down his beard."

Do you know who this faker was? It was King David. David needed a weapon. Here was the only one available. A priest had saved the sword of Goliath the Philistine, whom David had killed in the Valley of Elah. The priest gave it to David. "…And David said, There is none like that; give it to me." (I Samuel 21:9) This is the same sword of Goliath that he had used to cut off Goliath's head. (I Samuel 17:51)

There is more history to this story that is pertinent to our subject. David was fleeing from Saul and went to Gath where the Philistine king was named Achish. The problem arose when the people recognized David and began the famous saying, "Saul hath slain his thousands, and David his ten thousands." (I Samuel 21:11) The people then took David before the king Achish. Because of his fear David faked madness, and it worked. The king let him go, and he escaped. Achish said, "Lo, ye see the man is mad: wherefore then have ye brought him to me? Have I need of mad men?" (I Samuel 21:14,15)

Now read on. David, "escaped to the cave Adullam" and when his brethren and all his father's house heard it, they went down thither to him. And every one that was in distress, and every one that was in debt, and every one that was discontented, gathered themselves unto him; and he became a captain (leader) over them: and there were with him about four hundred men. (I Samuel 22:1,2) (If David had been a lawyer and arranged for the four hundred men to be placed on disability, he could have retired on his percentage of their disability checks.) However, David was not a lawyer, but a true leader and led the men back into productive activities.

II Samuel 14:2, 17, 19
And Joab sent a woman from Tekoah, to David with a message. Joab instructed the woman to feign mourning to get David's attention. David was able to discern good and bad and knew Joab had put the words in her mouth, and she confessed.

I Kings 14: 1,2, 5, 10, 17
The son of Jeroboam fell sick. Jeroboam asked his wife, to disguise herself, and go to the prophet Ahijah who was blind to plead for their son. God warned Ahijah and he said to her "why feignest thou thyself to be another?" She was informed that the child would die. God was bringing evil upon the house of Jeroboam because he had sinned and taken other gods and images.

Nehemiah 6:8
"Then I sent unto him, saying, There are no such things done as thou sayest, but thou feignest them out of thine own heart." Nehemiah was trying to build the wall around Jerusalem. The complaint was that the hard work would weaken them. (6:9) The ones against honest,

working, and knowledgeable people were recognized as fakers and the wall was completed.

Psalm 17:1
"Hear the right, O Lord, attend unto my cry, give ear unto my prayer, that goeth not out of feigned lips." David was aware of faked prayers without sincerity and was relating to God that he was sincere.

Jeremiah 3: 10, 11
"And yet for all this her treacherous sister Judah hath not turned unto me with her whole heart, but feignedly, saith the Lord. And the Lord said unto me, The backsliding Israel hath justified herself more than treacherous Judah." Both Israel and Judah sinned, but God judged Judah worse because they were faking goodness. Israel was openly sinning. (God condemns people who are faking goodness more than those who openly sin.)

Luke 20:20, 26
"And they watched him, and sent forth spies, which should **feign** themselves **just** men, that they might take hold of his words, that so they might deliver him unto the power and authority of the governor." Jesus, of course, knew they were fakes. They were "marveled" by His answer and shut up.

II Peter 2: 2,3
"And many shall follow their pernicious ways; by reason of whom **the way of truth** shall be evil spoken of. And through covetousness shall they with **feigned** words make merchandise of you: whose judgment now of a long time lingereth not, and their damnation slumbereth not."

I Timothy 5:3,6 (Read all of 5:3-15) NIV
"Give proper recognition to those widows who are really in need. But the widow who lives for pleasure is dead while she lives. Paul said beware of those who are "idle", "go from house to house", and are "gossips and busybodies." One of the most profound duties and commands for God's word is to support the needs of widows and

orphans. It is noted that even in Biblical times there were those who were fakes. In these modern times there are widows who are crooks. There are repeated stories of a widow moving in with a senile man and stealing all he has including his bank accounts and then disappearing. (One can assume such women were not abused and did not go "home to mother," but probably moved into a bigger house with another senile man.)

II Thessalonians 3: 10,11
"For even when we were with you, this we commanded you, that **if any would not work, neither should eat**. For we hear that there are some which walk among you disorderly, working not at all, but are busybodies." One can see these "busybodies" driving rapidly into a disabled parking place at a restaurant in a big shiny pickup truck with a large stainless steel tool chest on the truck next to the cab. They trot the first ten feet to the restaurant and limp the next thirty feet. (Sometimes they limp the first 10 feet and trot the last 30 feet.)

A friend described this experience to me. He was having dinner in a restaurant when he saw a man in his pick up truck with a disability sticker pull into a disabled parking space. Using his walking cane he walked slowly into the restaurant and sat down. Apparently he forgot something. He returned slowly to the pick-up truck without his cane. Suddenly, it began to rain. He ran like a track star back into the restaurant.

I have mentioned this scene for years to perhaps fifty people, and everyone has witnessed it and is disgusted by it. I have yet to meet a person who has not seen it.) The odds are that when one sees someone pull into a disability-parking place they are someone that should be walking more than they are. Many of them are close to the top of the fakes in America.

Ephesians 4:28

"Let him that stole steal no more: but rather let him labour, working with his hands the thing which is good, that he may have to give to him that needeth."

Matthew 25:26
Jesus said, "Thou wicked and slothful servant, thou knewest that I reap where I sowed not, and gather where I have not strewed:"

Proverbs 10:4, 5
"He becometh poor that dealeth with a slack hand: but the hand of the diligent maketh rich. He that gathereth in summer is a wise son: but he that sleepeth in harvest is a son that causeth shame."

Ephesians 4:14
The Apostle tells us of the "cunning craftiness of men, whereby they lie in wait to deceive."

Titus 1:10
" There are many unruly and vain talkers and deceivers…"

I Corinthians 15:33
"Be not deceived: evil communications corrupt good manners."

B.   Jewish Quotes

"Six days shalt thou work…" is a commandment as binding as the phrase which follows it, and on the seventh day thou shall rest." (Not work) (Mekhiltat on Exodus 20:9-10)

"For thou shalt eat the labor of thine hands…" (Psalm 128:2)

"The sleep of a laboring man is sweet, whether he eat little or much…" (Ecclesiastes 5:12)

"Idleness leads to immorality…and to degeneration." (Mishnah Ket. 5:5)

"Great is work for it leads to the dignity to man." (Neb. 49b.)

C.   Islam Quotes

The concept of work and labor is difficult to understand by studying reference books. In the nine books I have on Islam the word "work" or "labor" is not in any index. Socialism may be defined as the shared ownership and distribution of goods. (Webster) Zakat was instituted by Islam to offset the hoarding of wealth. This is a two and one-half percent tax on stationary capital. The idea is to increase the general wealth of humankind. (Any accountant can show that if this were consistently applied to hoarded wealth Zakat would "eat it up" in one generation.) This puts wealth back into production for more jobs, etc. One can see that Zakat is Socialism in Religious dress. Some relate Zakat to Almsgiving. Almsgiving means "purification" and cleanses the Muslim of greed or selfishness. Muslims are not to charge interest when loaning money to the needy. They are urged to give more. This is known as Sadaquah and is different from Zakat because it is voluntary. However, with all this, it is said that every Muslim desires and plans to become a "millionaire".

Even though I could not find the word "work" in their vocabulary, it is also noted that they overexert themselves to become rich. A firm rule is that they do not cheat fellow humans to obtain wealth. Every person should obtain his own. Every person is expected to contribute to the community as a whole. The term "disability" is also not in their vocabulary, but they are expected to help the needy.

Chapter IV.
Quotes from the Interlinear Hebrew Old Testament Bible

John R. Kohlenberger III, Zondervan Publishing House, 1987:

Proverbs 6: 5-12, 15
"Free yourself like a gazelle from the hand of the hunter, like a bird from the snare of the fowler." (v. 5)

"Go to the ant, you sluggard; consider its ways, and be wise!" (v. 6)

"It has no commander, no overseer, or ruler." (v.7)

"Yet it stores its provisions in the summer, and gathers its food at harvest." (v. 8)

"How long will you lie there you sluggard? When will you get up from your sleep?" (v. 9)

"A little sleep, a little slumber, a little folding of the hands to rest and poverty will come on you like a bandit and scarcity like an armed man." (v. 10)

"A scoundrel and villain who foes about with a corrupt mouth... Therefore disaster will overtake him in an instant; he will suddenly be destroyed without remedy." (v. 12)

Proverbs 10:26

"As vinegar to the teeth, and as smoke to the eyes, so is the sluggard to them that send him."

Proverbs 19: 23-26
"The fear of the Lord leads to life: Then one rests content, untouched by trouble… The sluggard (lazy) buries his hand in the dish; he will not even bring it back to his mouth." (v. 23, 24)

"Flog a mocker and the simple will learn providence, rebuke a discerning man, and he will gain knowledge. He who robs his father and drives out his mother is a son who brings shame and disgrace." (v. 25,26)

Proverbs 26:16
"The lazy man is wiser in his own eyes than seven men who answer discretely."

Proverbs 30:25
"Ants are creatures of little strength, yet they store up their food in the summer."

Chapter V.
Quotes from Early Historians: (19)

Clement of Alexander (153-193 –220 A.D.?)
"After Justin and Irenaeus he is the founder of Christian literature."
(p. 163)

"Alexander is the brain of Christendom: its heart was yet beating at Antioch." The west was receptive only, but looking for further enlightenment. **(p.163)**

He is the immediate precursor of the Gospel. **(p. 166)**

St. Jerome says he is "most learned of the ancients."

Eusebius says, "He is an incomparable of Christian philosophy." He succeeded Pantaenus as the head of the Catechetical School at Alexandria. He did a missionary tour to the East about 189 A.D. His life was to win pagans to the Christian faith. He taught a code of Christian morals and manners. A manual for the "whole duty of men." He noted society was tainted by "incredible licentiousness and luxury." **(p. 167)** He taught the true God from the inspired scriptures. He wrote a classic on *"Who is the Rich Man That Shall be Saved?"* He related that the Lord did not require the renunciation of worldly goods, but the disposition of the soul is the great essential." **(p. 169)**

He describes "yawning" as the body falling down and soft beds as "being a lazy contrivance for rest." **(p. 257)** He said the soul does not need sleep and napping in the day, stretching, yawning, and other fits of uselessness were frivolous manifestations of uneasiness of soul" **(p. 259)** He quotes I Corinthians 15:33 as "evil communication, corrupt good manners." **(p. 314)** He says that " a man who does not take precaution against a theft, or does not prevent it, he is the cause of it, and to prevent attaches the blame of what happens." **(p. 319)** He quotes Ephesians 4:28: "Let him that stole steal no more: but rather let him labour, working with his hands the thing which is good, that he may have to give to him that needeth." **(p. 321)** (Pay taxes so others can have.)

"We treat things different, indifferently, and in much feebleness nurture indulging ourselves. It is the business of bad spiritual powers to make their own those who have renounced them." **(p. 371)**

Clement quotes Agatho, a pagan, to reveal how we may distort our activities: "Treating our by-work as work, and doing our work as by-work." He said these people were "called thieves by the Lord." **(p. 475)**

Clement further quotes Parmenides: "For thinking and being are the same." And Aristophanes as: "For to think and to do are equivalent." **(p. 485)**

Chapter VI.
Quotes From Early Historians (20) and Others:

A.   Quotes from Early Historians (20)

Tertullian (145-20A.D.) a great founder of Latin Christianity said, "Covetousness is the root of all evils." He quotes Paul, "… covetousness, which is idolatry." (Colossians 3:5)

By false swearing one becomes a minister of covetousness. (Idolatry) Covetousness reveals the selfish motive for acquiring something. Those who aid in the production of idols are idolaters just as those who supported and trained gladiators were murderers. Those who by false swearing show they have not learned to respect life and show a denial of God. **(p. 67)** Tertullian said, "The apples of Sodom and Gomorrah if touched turn to ashes." **(p. 48)**

Psammetichus suggested that Christians are the "third race". Some Christians have abandoned the education of their children. We must be producing a "fourth race." **(p. 116, 643)**

Tertullian, "There is nothing so old as the truth." **(p. 51)**

B.   Other Quotes

Charles Finney, (1792-1875) one of the greatest of the early American preachers was talking about the Kingdom of God, but he made an interesting statement, "Every member must work or quit. No honorary members." **(23, p. 255)**

Benjamin Franklin said, "God helps them that helps themselves." **(23, p. 239)**

Alexander Hamilton, (1755-1804) said, " A power over a man's support is a power over his will." **(24, p. 171)**

"There is no such thing as a free lunch." (**Anonymous**) **(24, p. 173)**

Georgia O'Keeffe, (1887-1986) said, "To be an American one must feel America, like America, love America and _**work**_." (24, p. 345)

Joseph Conrad, "A man is a worker. If he is not that he is nothing." **(30, p. 311)**

Robert Frost, "The world is filling with willing people: Some willing to work, the rest willing to let them." **(30, p. 311)**

Orville Dewey, "Work is a man's greatest function: He is nothing, he can do nothing, he can achieve nothing, he can fulfill nothing, _**without work**_." **(30, p. 145)**

Theodore Roosevelt, "It is only through work that we move on to better things." **(30, p. 146)**

William Blake, "No bird soars too high if he soars with his own wings." **(30, p. 11)**

Booker T. Washington, "You can't hold a man down without staying down with him." **(30, p. 13)**

Ralph Waldo Emerson, "Hitch your wagon to a star." **(30, p. 12)**

"In the sweat of thy face shalt thou eat bread, till thou return unto the ground?" (Grave) (Genesis 3:19) **(25, p. 314)**

"Work is the duty of all citizens." (A Russian quote) **(25, p. 314)**

Lewis Morris, "Work is the law of life and its best fruit." **(25, p. 314)**

John Chrysostom, "Work our share lest we should make this world our rest and not hope for the hereafter." **(25, p. 315)**

Stanislous, "Laziness, a premature death." **(25, p. 323)**

"Laziness, the metal alertness to avoid hard work." **(Anonymous) (25, p. 323)**

Thinking is: **(25, p. 570)**
- "As he thinketh in his heart, so is he." (Proverbs 23:7)
- "To converse with oneself." (Miguel de Unamuno)
- "The magic of the mind." (Lord Byron)
- "The hardest work there is." (Henry Ford)
- "The talking of the soul with self." (Plato)
- "The only thing one can do when not working that can be fruitful." (Michel de Montaigne)

Work is: **(25, pp. 615, 616)**
- "The most dignified thing in the life of men." (Ben-Gurion)
- "A life of ease is not for any man." (Thomas Carlisle)
- "The measure of civilization. Savages do not work." (Calvin Coolidge)
- "The salvation of the race." (Henry Ford)
- "Love made visible." (Kahlil Gibran)
- "The saviors of society." (Eugene V. Debs)
- "To serve God in his calling." (Richard Steele)

Epictetus (50-125 A.D.) "Sickness is a hindrance to the body, but not to the will, unless the will consents." **(42, p. 684)**

Xenophon (430-358 B.C.) "Cowards under stress were recognized as natural slaves." **(42, p. 780)**

This large number of quotes from great men of the past support the evils of the worker who will not work!

Chapter VII.
Low Back Pain History and Evaluation

One must be able to recognize pathology to know when it is not present.
(**Sections VII – XI** are for physicians only, but may be scanned by others for a concept of the complexity of the problem.)

A.   Introduction

Moses related bad backs as "crookback, and hunchback." (Leviticus 21:20)

King David complained of back pain: "The plowers plowed upon my back; they made their long furrows." (Psalm 129:3) "My back is filled with searing pain." (NIV, Psalm 38:7)

Shakespeare described back pain in graphic terms several times; "load o' gravel i' th' back, sciaticas", "thou cold sciatica, cripple our senator".

Leewenhoek (1707): "As long as I sit still I am without any pain, but if I do but walk little I have pains in my legs".

Hippocrates: "There are many varieties of curvature of the spine even in persons in good health; for it takes place from natural conformation and from pains, in movement of the body when everyone begins to endure pain, it will be relieved by rest".

Contractures of the back usually not accompanied by an objective sign of a lesion of the nervous system have been described in 1915 as simple kyphosis, kyphoscoliosis, vertebral curvature, vertebral analgesic attitudes, (Sicard) traumatic kyphosis, spondylitis, contracture of the adnominal muscles (flexions of the spine), and Camptocormia (Souques). Even though not described in 1915, but clearly shown in their figure is a patient with Camptocormia, which includes not only flexion of the spine, but also flexion of the upper and lower extremities. In the cases I have seen the patient always walked in the room with the body flexed as well as flexion of the elbows, wrists, hips, and knees. Nothing else looks like this. It is very non-organic and easily proved to be so by an experienced examiner. (10, p. 61, 62) There is no disease process that causes this picture.

B. The Magnitude of the Problem of Back Pain:

Back pain is second only to upper respiratory infections as a cause for lost time from work. (1, p. 3) Back pain may be described as the "Megabucks Syndrome", for it is estimated that back disorders cost U.S industry 35 billion dollars a year by 1990. (1, p. 6) 45% of this cost is related to permanent disability payments. (1, p. 7) Back injuries involve between 50% and 80% of the adult working population at some time during their lives. (1, p. 3) Back injuries account for 23% of all cases involving disability (1, p. 5)

There are three factors in morality. This includes the **society morality**, the **individual morality**, and the **religious morality**.

The actions of society morality in a government based on the concept of church and state separation cannot be motivated by religious interest, but must be derived by the needs of the community as a whole. Every government system has had some method of taking care of the poor. The power of government comes from God as do all powers and is one of the greatest blessings when the government programs take care of people who cannot take care of themselves for one reason or the other. This book supports these programs, and this author is proud to be a part of it. The problem arises with the immorality of politics. It is obvious that politics is driven by votes, and **votes are driven by people with or without morals.** The abuse of disability programs is the subject of this book. **The number of people who abuse of the blessings of government disability programs is known to be in the millions**. That group of abusers is not only abusing others who are supporting them, but the greatest tragedy is the destruction of their own character and personal worth to society. The excess financial burden brought on by the "fakers" causes a limitation of funds to be available to those who need and deserve it.

We all share sympathy for the truly disabled. If the unworthy were eliminated from the budget, more would be available for the true ones in need. Malingering, which is fraud, is so widespread that it influences the whole system.

C.   The Answer to The Problem:

The answer is the prevention of fake claims for disability. In my conversations with a wide segment of people I have yet to talk with someone who was not appalled at faking disability. Therefore, the **first** step in prevention is to inform the medical profession that they must be aware of the *extensive nature of the problem*. **Secondly,** they must *educate themselves* to recognize it. **Thirdly**, the legal profession must *eliminate the so-called "legal disability mills"* that make promises to get disability for those who have been turned down. Computerization should be able to raise a special flag for those once turned down. This should put them in a special group to be evaluated by medical, government, and legal experts in the field of medical complaint. There is no doubt that mistakes are made both ways. **A second review will do two things. It will reassure those with real disability and identify again those who are malingering.**

The public needs to be aroused to report those on disability who show it is not deserved. The working men and women must get involved with those abusing them. The medical and legal profession should become more alert, honest, intelligent, and courageous in turning down any person who is trying to commit fraud against the government and their fellow man. ***Sympathy to the bad side of human nature should be eliminated.***

There are many medical problems that can be faked to obtain disability, but this book will deal only with that of **back pain.** The author has considerable experience with evaluating the disability and faked disability caused by back pain. A standardized approach is presented. Back pain accounts for a large percentage of the money spent on disability for two reasons. First, there are many cases. Second, back pain does not kill you. These individuals can live a long time and are paid for years and years.

Back pain is an **Old Problem**, a **Big Problem**, and may become **Your Problem**. Back pain is an **Old** problem that has been present since Biblical days. It is a **Big** Problem. Eighty percent of workers at some point in their lives will have back pain. It represents 24% of all cases of disability. The cost is thought to be 35 billion dollars each year. It may become **Your** problem. It affects the most productive people of society usually at middle age. It is worse and more common in smokers. It is more common in those who have poor physical conditions.

Eighty percent of back injured workers return to work in three weeks. The treatment is limited and includes bed rest, mild drugs, and flexion exercises.

The development of CT scans and MRI's has increased the accuracy of the diagnosis of the causes of organic back pain, but has escalated the cost.

Back pain affects the most productive people of society. The highest incidence of back pain is found among construction workers, truck drivers, and nurses. (**1, p. 8, 9**) This is particularly true in women in construction work. (Lynch, personal communication).

D.   Associated Factors:

Lifting:

Lifting accounts for 75% of the injuries and 50% of these individuals were lifting at least 60 lbs. **(I, p. 9)** The number of lifts per day has not been determined to be important since 20% of the injuries were the first lift of the day. **(1, p. 10)** Slipping, twisting, and falling accounts for up to 42% of the injuries. **(1, p. 11)**

Physical Condition:

Good physical fitness is important in prevention of injuries, as injuries are ten times more common in the least fit group. **(1, p. 11)** Interestingly, however, data do not support obesity as a factor as is commonly believed. **(1, p. 15)**

Age:

The average age of back injuries is 36. **(1, p. 13)**

Attitude:

Level of job satisfaction is important. Studies have shown that unhappy workers are more prone to suffer from low back pain syndromes than are workers who have a high degree of satisfaction with their work environment. **(1, p. 13)**

Smoking:

Back pain is increased among smokers. **(1, p. 14)** An increased intra discal pressure has been noted. The pain is frequently thought to be more severe in smokers. The effect of chronic coughing may be a factor.

Pre-Employment Physicals:

Data do not support the efficiency of pre-employment physicals and screening in reducing the incidence of low back injuries. Pre-employment back x-rays are likewise ineffective and are not recommended. **(1, p. 16)**

Back History:

The only probable predictor of back trouble is a history of previous back trouble. **(1, p. 16)**

Strength Testing:
Pre-employment strength testing as related to job requirements seems effective in reducing back injuries. **(1, p. 18)**

Light Duty:
The availability of a light work status is important in reducing time off and expediting return to full function. Companies that do not permit this can expect a deleterious effect on lost time injuries. Prolonged absence has a profound psychological effect. Workers off six months have only a 50% chance of ever returning to productive work. When off for a year this drops to 25% and when off two years return to work is rare. **(1, p. 22)**

The guidelines as established by the American Medical Association, the American Academy of Orthopedic Surgeons, the Veterans Administration, and the Social Security Administration are of little help to the evaluator when it comes to rating any specific low back injury in our experience as well as others. **(1, p. 715)**

Early Evaluation:
Review of each back injury during the first week of injury by a designated back specialist who understands standards of care and frequently scheduled reviews has been shown to reduce cost and decrease the return to work time. **(1, p. 26)**

An accurate diagnosis of the scientific etiology of back pain cannot be made with the first attack in many cases. When a diagnosis is made, it is usually related to the intervertebral disc, facet joints, or is classified as a muscular strain. One third of those with chronic back pain will develop sciatica, and one-half will develop cervical pain in their lives. **(1, p. 44)**

X-ray evidence of disc degeneration is seen in 83% of adults. **(1, p. 45)** However, in a study of pure compressive loading there was no difference in the failure of a degenerative disc from a normal disc. **(1, p. 49)**

E. Classification of the Common Causes of Back Pain: (Miller)

By scanning any textbook of internal medicine, one can readily list over 100 conditions that occasionally have associated back pain. I have developed a classification of 27 of the most common causes of back pain, all of which will be seen over a period of time in a back clinic. These 27 most common causes are divided into 9 groups of 3 each and include: the Big 3, Inflammations, Malignant Tumors, Benign Tumors, Metabolic Causes, Fractures, Structural Abnormalities, Infections, and Referred Back Pain.

A CLASSIFICATION OF THE 27 MOST COMMON CAUSES OF BACK PAIN
(Divided into 9 groups of 3 each.)

1. Big 3
2. Inflammations
3. Malignant Tumors

4. Benign Tumors
5. Metabolic Causes
6. Structural Abnormalities

7: Fractures
8. Infections
9. Referred Pains

F.   27 MOST COMMON CAUSES OF BACK PAIN

Big 3
1. Back Strain
2. Herniated Disc
    3. Degenerative Spine Disease a. Spondylosis b. Facet syndrome c. Spinal stenosis

3 Inflammations
1. Ankylosing Spondylitis
2. Rheumatoid Arthritis
3. Polymyalgia Rheumatica

3 Malignant Tumors
1. Multiple Myeloma
2. Lymphomas
3. Metastatic Tumors

3 Benign Tumors
1. Osteoid Osteoma
2. Osteochondroma
3. Giant Cell Tumor

3 Metabolic
1. Osteoporosis
2. Sickle Cell Crisis
3. Gout

3 Structural Abnormalities
1. Spondylolysis
2. Spondylolisthesis
3. Idiopathic Scoliosis

3 Fractures
1. Compression Fracture
2. Burst Fracture
3. Fracture Dislocation

(facets, transverse process, etc.)

Infections: 3 Acute, 3 Chronic

Acute
1. Acute hematogenous osteomyelitis
2. Pyogenic Discitis or Post-operative Discitis
3. Epidural Abscess

Chronic
1. Osteomyelitis
2. Tuberculosis
3. Fungi

3 Referred:
1. Abdominal Aortic Aneurysm
2. Genitourinary
3. Gastrointestinal

G. The Outline of the Clinical Evaluation of Low Back Pain:

The clinical evaluation of low back pain requires certain specific information from the history and physical examination, and *correlation* of these findings with appropriate diagnostic tests. This will assist in establishing the correct diagnosis and treatment plan and gives the patient the best assurance of returning to productive employment and happy leisure activities.

It is to be noted that in large studies most with low back injuries do return to work. In 12,000 compensation cases studied, 80% were back at work in three weeks and 90% in six weeks. **(1, p. 21)** Therefore, the evaluation should not be an "overkill" and include expensive studies and treatment that might be counterproductive.

I have used the following outline for almost twenty years in evaluating the patient clinically. It provides the minimal pertinent information needed. Additional information will be required in certain cases. Each section of the outline may be elaborated on as the specifics of the individual case demand.

LOW BACK PAIN CLINICAL EVALUATION OUTLINE

I. History:
1. Mechanical Back Pain (See discussion)
2. Sciatica (See discussion)
   Conservative treatment a. Bed rest b. Physical therapy - exercises c. Drugs

II. Examination:
   1. **Back** a. Shape: Kyphosis, Lordosis, Scoliosis b. Mobility: Spasm, Segmentation, Excursion c. Tenderness: Point Percussion or Compression

   2. **Neurologic** a. Motor: Reflexes, Weakness b. Sensory: Sensory and Pain Distribution c. SLR, cross, + SLR
   3. **Diagnostic Tests**

III. Determination of the Indications for Disc Surgery:
The indication for surgery includes characteristic incapacitating mechanical back and sciatic pain supported by findings with appropriate abnormal diagnostic tests and not relieved by adequate conservative treatment.

H. BACK PAIN CLINICAL EVALUATION:

1. History:
There are three things in the history that must be evaluated to get a good understanding of the individual patient's problem.

a. Mechanical Back Pain:

One must establish whether or not the patient has mechanical back pain. This means pain that is made worse by certain activities and made better by certain positions. A constant boring, persistent pain not related to activities or position has a different differential diagnosis than mechanical pain.

b. Sciatic Pain:

One must establish whether or not sciatic pain is part of the problem. The word leg pain is not used in writing up the history. The establishment of sciatic pain as posterolateral pain in the hip, thigh, and pain to the calf presents a different differential diagnosis than pain that is in the groin radiating to the anterior medial thigh to the knee. Pain that does not go below the knee is not true sciatica. A patient with true sciatic pain is less likely to respond to conservative therapy than one complaining of back pain only. The specific location of back and leg pain in herniated disc lesions is helpful in establishing the level of the herniation. Back pain in L4 disc herniations is often referred to the sacroiliac area, and the leg pain radiates to the anterorlateral aspect of the lower leg and to the dorsum of foot and great toe. In L5 disc over S 1 root lesions, back pain often radiates to the greater trochanter and sometimes groin; and the radicular component radiates to the posterior calf, heel and plantar aspect of the foot.

c. Conservative Treatment:

The type, effect and amount of conservative therapy must be noted in the history. (It is ludicrous to recommend bed rest and physical therapy to a patient who has had this already. I have seen such a hundred times. The motivation is a lack of diagnosis and being too busy to try to solve the problem.) The trend must be established as to whether or not the patient is improving. The drug intake must be carefully evaluated. It is not rare to see a patient who is taking 8-15 pills per day. (This may be appropriate in rheumatoid arthritis patients taking aspirin.) The individual who is taking pain medicine 6- 8 times a day for six months to a year must be considered dependent on that medication. That fact must be taken into account in the patient's treatment. If a "**Tens Unit**" helps that is considered a non-organic result for a mechanical nerve root problem.

2. Examination:

The examination includes three major categories: the back exam, neurologic findings, and specific tests.

a. Back Exam:

In examining the back, one frequently notes that the patient walks with an antalgic gait, which is a flexion type of posture favoring the painful leg. The shape of the back including the loss of normal lordosis, kyphosis or scoliosis is noted. Spastic scoliosis is common in acute disc rupture due to pain and reflex splinting. It is also seen in other acute clinical back problems. In the acute phase of a back strain or disc herniation the lumbar spine is frequently rigid. Pain on extension is seen in lumbar stenosis, acute disc rupture and facet disease. Sciatic pain on extending suggests a nerve root problem. When lumbosacral pain is only reproduced on extension, one suspects facet disease. Diffuse lumbar tenderness may be related to functional problems. Localized percussion tenderness may be significant in level localization. Have the patient bend forward until sciatic pain is produced and then raise up until it subsides and the individual spines are percussed. It is considered positive for localization when sciatic pain is reproduced at the level percussed.

b. Neurologic Exam:

Determining the level of neurologic impairment involves correlation of motor and sensory findings and diagnostic imaging techniques. The motor evaluation includes testing of reflexes and muscle strength. The L4 and L5 roots are most likely involved in lumbar stenosis, and the L5 and S1 roots are most involved in herniated nucleus pulposus. The knee jerk is depressed in an L4 root lesion, and the ankle jerk is depressed in an S1 root lesion. Weakness of the quadriceps is seen in the L4 root lesion. Weakness of the anterior tibial and extensor hallucis longus is characteristic of an L5 root lesion. The S1 root lesion causes a weakness of the extensor digitorum brevis and gastrosoleus complex. Muscles are frequently innervated by multiple roots, thus weakness may not be present.

The sensory evaluation is frequently not reliable, but in a specific case may be quite accurate. The L4 root produces numbness more anterior in the thigh and anteromedially at the knee. Numbness that extends to the large toe indicates an L5 root lesion. Numbness that extends to the base of the small toe or heel points to the S1 root lesion. The numbness may be diffuse and poorly localized across the foot, and therefore, has no root-specific localizing value.

Straight leg raising is the single most important positive finding in the diagnosis of a surgical lesion. This is present in 97% of young patients with a herniated nucleus pulposus involving the L5 or S1 root. Thus, it is extremely rare to have a herniated disc in which this test is not clearly positive. It is usually positive in patients with spinal stenosis who require surgery. The contralateral straight leg raising test is an extremely accurate test for a ruptured disk as it is virtually never seen in other clinical problems. This involves straight leg raising of the asymptomatic leg and producing pain in the contralateral or symtomatic leg or hip.

3.   Specific Tests:

Currently the imaging study of choice for most spine problems includes the CT scan and the MRI. However, it is still not rare to find the individual with nerve root compression in which the exact pathology is not seen with current techniques. Imaging occasionally reveals multiple abnormalities that may not fit clinically. The incidence of false positives and false negatives continues to haunt us. However, with use of the CT scans, myelography, and particularly post myelogram CT scan and MRI, one should demonstrate pathology in most cases. In contrast to times past surgery is rarely indicated with adequate and technically good imaging. The exception may be an extremely obese patient.

Plain lumbar spine x-rays:
These are useful in structural problems, in diagnosis of spondylosis, degenerative disc disease, spondylolysis, spondylolisthesis, tumors, and fractures. It is also helpful in measuring the canal dimensions in spinal stenosis. An AP diameter of the lumbar spinal canal of less

than 11mm is abnormal, and a transverse diameter of less than 25mm is considered abnormal in the adult.

Myelograms:
For many, the myelogram is considered the procedure of choice in evaluating spinal stenosis because it readily evaluates multiple levels. It is also very useful in the diagnosis of disc herniation and intraspinal mass lesions. It is particularly helpful when used in conjunction with the CT scan.

Computerized Tomography (CT Scan):
CT is useful in the evaluation of a variety of disorders including disc herniation, spinal stenosis, and tumors. It is frequently used in conjunction with a myelogram as an "enhanced CT scan".

MRI:
The MRI is very accurate in tumors and congenital abnormalities that involve the spinal cord. It is becoming the initial procedure of choice for most spine lesions.

Chapter VIII.
Specific Diagnostic Categories:

Big 3:

1.   Lumbar Strain:
The back pain may be acute or chronic. It is nonradiating and may include the buttocks and posterior thigh. The etiology is muscular, ligamentous, a tear in the annulus, or facet disease. It is usually classified into mild, moderate and severe with recovery being in 1,2 or 3 weeks respectively. X-rays are not done initially. Treatment is bedrest, exercises and return to normal function as quickly as possible. Drug treatment is nonsteroidal anti-inflammatory drugs (NSAID). Recovery is complete except in chronic cases.

2.   Herniated Disc:
Mechanical back pain with sciatica is usually present. The examination reveals back and nerve root findings. The diagnosis is confirmed by the appropriate imaging of the CT scan, myelogram or MRI. With conservative treatment most recover. Our patients have had a certain amount of screening and treatment, yet **90%** with the syndrome either recover or the symptoms are not severe enough to warrant surgery. Treatment is bedrest at home, NSAID or a short course of steroids. Codeine is used if needed for pain. Valium is contraindicated since it is a depressant. Surgery will usually be successful if appropriate criteria for selection of surgical candidates are utilized.

3. Degenerative Spine Disease:
a. Spondylosis: Spondylosis is a general term for the degenerative

spine disease of osteoarthritis. In later years this is present in most of the population.

b. Facet Syndrome*:* The pain is in the back often with associated posterior buttock, proximal posterior thigh or groin radiation. It is made worse by sitting, standing, and particularly extension of the back; and is better with bed rest. Relief by facet blocks further supports the diagnosis.

c. Spinal Stenosis:

Symptoms include pain and paresthesias and may be mild or severely incapacitating. The usual picture is the inability to walk more than a short distance because of buttock or leg pain. Walking downhill is more difficult because this causes spinal extension. Sitting, flexing forward, or lying relieves the pain. The patient may ride a bicycle because this causes flexion of the spine and yet be unable to walk more than a short distance. The sine qua non of determining the difference between a spinal claudication and a vascular claudication is the presence of good pulses in the spinal claudication group. Vascular claudication localizes the pain more clearly to the calves, which is cramping, and is readily relieved when one stops walking and rests. Paresthesias are usually not present. Walking uphill is more difficult than downhill because of the increased energy required. A classic finding is the absence of pulses. Imaging for stenosis includes plain x-rays for the measurement of canal diameter, a myelogram and enhanced CT scanning. Surgery is indicated only when the pain is incapacitating and not relieved by conservative management. Conservative treatment includes use of NSAID (non-steroidal inflammatory drugs) and occasional lumbar epidural blocks.

The 3 Inflammations:

1. Ankylosing Spondylitis:

If the following five criteria are met, the diagnosis for ankylosing spondylitis should be strongly considered: (1) the onset is insidious, (2) it occurs before age 40, (3) it persists for more than three months, (4) there is morning stiffness, and (5) the patient is better with exercise. The pain may be mild to severe. The examination may show a loss of lordosis with tender sacroiliac joints. Twenty-five percent of the patients have iritis. The sedimentation rate is increased and the HIA-B27 is positive in 90% of the cases. X-rays reveal active sclerosis at the sacroiliac joints, squaring of vertebral bodies, calcification of the anterior longitudinal ligament, and the bone scan is positive. The treatment is NSAID especially Butazolidin. The course may be benign but is usually disabling.

2.   Rheumatoid Arthritis:

This is a disease that involves small joints, including hands, feet, wrists, elbows, hips, knees, ankles and the spine. The lumbar spine is involved in later stages. The syndrome is one of pain, stiffness that is worse in the morning and associated fatigue. Laboratory studies reveal anemia, increased sedimentation rate, and rheumatoid factors are present in 80% of the patients. One cannot predict the outcome in an early stage.

3.   Polymyalgia Rheumatica:

The syndrome is severe stiffness, tenderness and aching in the proximal upper and lower extremities. The age is usually over 50 and women are most often affected. The laboratory tests show an increased sedimentation rate in almost every case. One-third have an abnormal liver function test. The pain is worse in the morning and there is difficulty getting up. There is associated fever, fatigue and weight loss. There is a dramatic response to steroids. If a headache is present, one must evaluate for jaw claudication and visual changes, and if present, there is an associated arteritis. The treatment of arteritis is steroids to prevent blindness. The patient should be on low dose steroids for at least two years. The patient is better within five days, and the sedimentation rate rapidly returns to normal in most cases.

The 3 Malignant Tumors:

1.   Multiple Myeloma

Multiple myeloma is a malignant tumor of plasma cells. It is the most common primary bone tumor in adults. Patients are usually over age 50, and low back pain is the presenting complaint in

35% of cases. Laboratory tests reveal an anemia, a leukocytosis, a thrombocytopenia, a positive Coombs test, hypercalcemia, hyperuricemia, and increased creatinine. The alkaline phosphatase is normal. There is Bence-Jones protein in the urine. The diagnosis is by bone marrow aspirate. X-rays reveal multiple osteolytic lesions. The treatment is melphalan plus steroids and the average survival is five years.

2. Lymphomas:

Lymphomas cause bone pain, which is worse in bed and is made worse by alcohol. The diagnosis is verified when the pathological diagnosis of lymphoma is made. Hodgkin's lymphoma occasionally presents in an adult with back pain. In non-Hodgkin's lymphoma presentation of back pain is rare. Radiation and / or chemotherapy may be effective. A cure is possible in localized lesions.

3. Metastases:

The metastatic tumor syndrome is back pain associated with prior history of malignancy, but not uncommonly the first presentation of a malignancy is skeletal metastasis. The most common primary sites are prostate, lung, breast, kidney, thyroid and colon. In younger individuals neuroblastoma, Ewing's sarcoma and osteogenic sarcoma are also to be considered. These tumors are generally considered to be primary.

The 3 Benign Tumors

1. Osteoid Osteoma

This is a benign tumor seen in young adults that characteristically causes pain at night and is readily relieved by aspirin. (I remember a seventeen year old who had been given codeine for pain. He was not relieved. He went to visit his grandmother who gave him two aspirin that completely relieved his pain. This is almost a diagnostic test.) The x-ray reveals a sclerotic lesion with radiolucent center, which is revealed on a CT scan and bone scan. The lumbosacral spine is the most common spinal location. There is associated spasm and scoliosis. In fact, one should suspect this lesion in a young adult who first develops scoliosis. The treatment is excision.

2. Osteochondroma
The osteochondroma is also benign. It may become very large and compress the neural structures. The laboratory exam is normal. X-rays reveal a bony mass, which may be pedunculated or sessile. If asymptomatic it may be observed. Treatment is excision. Malignant transformation is uncommon.

3. Giant Cell Tumor
The giant cell tumor, rarely curative, is aggressive and may become malignant. The laboratory tests are normal but one needs calcium, phosphorous, alkaline phosphatase to exclude hyperparathyroidism and Paget's disease. X-rays reveal an expansile lytic lesion. The treatment is en block excision when possible. If total removal is not accomplished, the recurrence rate is over 50%. Radiation therapy is also indicated..

The 3 Metabolic Causes

1. Osteoporosis
In bone density studies over 50% of women above 65 have it. In 3% of the cases it is progressive and disabling and may be associated with drugs such as Heparin, anticonvulsants (Dilantin) and Methotrexate. It can be asymptomatic to severely painful with fractures. The fracture pain lasts up to three months or may be permanent. The laboratory tests are normal and the X-rays are characteristic. The bone scan is positive if fractures are present. The treatment for the fracture is bed rest for at least one week, analgesics and sometimes bracing. Medical treatment remains controversial and largely ineffective.

2. Gout
Back pain is seen in long-standing gout in individuals more than 50 years of age. The laboratory tests reveal hyperuricemia. X-ray reveals a cystic erosion of the ilium, sacrum and endplates of the

vertebrae. The treatment is Allopurinol for chronic maintenance and Indomethacin for the acute attacks of pain.

3. Sickle Cell Anemia
The syndrome is seen in African-Americans with diffuse back, bone, and abdominal pain with anemia, a positive smear for sickle cell and abnormal hemoglobin, and electrophoresis. The treatment is analgesics, antibiotics, and occasionally exchange transfusions.

The 3 Structural Abnormalities

1. Spondylolysis
Spondylolysis is seen in 5% of people over age 17. The lesion is in the pars interarticularis, and the etiology is thought to be repeated small stress fractures during the rapid growth period. It may or may not be symptomatic.

2. Spondylolisthesis
In 50% of the cases that become symptomatic, an injury is not identified. Increased slippage is very rare after age 20 unless there has been an injury or surgery. The pain is mechanical back pain. One can frequently palpate displacement and malalignment of the posterior spine involved. Range of motion is frequently normal, but there may be some restriction of extension. Imaging by lateral spine x-rays reveals the extent of the slipping, and the oblique x-ray reveals the defect in the pars. The treatment is the same as other back problems. Surgery is indicated only for incapacitating pain. Once spondylolisthesis becomes symptomatic the patient is usually unable to return to heavy work.

3. Idiopathic Scoliosis
When the diagnosis is made, prompt referral to an orthopedic specialist is indicated. This is particularly true with children.

The 3 Fractures

1. Compression Fracture

2. Burst Fracture

3. Fracture Dislocation (facets, transverse process, etc.)

The diagnosis of the 3 fracture syndromes is made by a history of trauma with x-ray confirmation.

The Infections: - 3 Acute, 3 Chronic

Infections of the lumbar spine may be acute or chronic. The diagnosis is important because when detected early the treatment is frequently curative.

Acute

1. Acute Hematogenous Vertebral Osteomyelitis

Acute vertebral hematogenous osteomyelitis is caused by a variety of organisms frequently originating from infections from the urinary tract, retrosigmoid area, or post partum infections.

2. Discitis

Pyogenic Discitis - Pyogenic discitis is uncommon but may be seen following intercurrent infection. The patient presents with fever, a rigid painful back, and an increased sedimentation rate. The diagnosis is by **MRI** with contrast, bone scan, and identification of the organism by needle biopsy, which is negative 50% of the time. (Beware, the pain may be diffuse from the lower thoracic to the sacral area. I remember a young patient with a negative MRI that only covered the lumbar area to the mid portion of L,1. A week later it was repeated and the discitis was clearly shown at T12.) The treatment is appropriate antibiotics, immobilization with bedrest, and bracing. Most patients recover.

Post Operative Discitis - Post operative discitis follows removal of a lumbar disc manifested by recurrent severe pain and spasm, verified by increased sedimentation rate, **MRI** with contrast, positive bone scan, biopsy and identification of the organism. The treatment is the same as pyogenic discitis.

3. Epidural Spinal Abscess

Epidural abscesses are probably becoming more common. They usually follow some other infection and may be associated with a postoperative discitis. The patient has severe back pain and may have a progressive neurological deficit. The patient is usually febrile with an increased sedimentation rate. X-rays usually reveal a site of primary infection. The diagnosis is made by CT scan or MRI. Treatment is biopsy and identification of the organism with bed rest, antibiotics and immobilization by bracing. If a neurological deficit is present and progressive, then emergency decompression is indicated.

The 3 Chronic
1. Osteomyelitis
2. Tuberculosis
3. Fungi

Chronic osteomyelitis of the spine may be: (a) bacterial, (b) tuberculosis, or (c) fungal. Diagnosis is suggested by chronic back pain, local findings, and appropriate diagnostic studies. Fever may or may not be present. Laboratory evaluation usually reveals an increased sedimentation rate, and aspiration specimens or biopsies may be culture positive for the infecting organism. Treatment is with appropriate antibiotics, bedrest, and immobilization. Early diagnosis of infective lesions may prevent their becoming chronic. Surgical decompression is indicated in progressive neurological deficits.

The 3 Referred

1. Abdominal Aortic Aneurysm
The abdominal aortic aneurysm syndrome is one of excruciating abdominal and back pain, and shock with an expanding abdominal mass. Diagnosis is made by ultrasound and CT scan. Treatment is emergency surgery. (Remember they all enlarge with time. A vascular consultation is indicated.)

2. Genitourinary Tract
The pain of the genitourinary tract is usually colicky, localized to the flank, suprapubic or perineal area (depending on whether or not the kidney, bladder or prostate is involved) and is associated with fever and other signs of infection.

3. Gastrointestinal Tract

Pain is referred to the back from the duodenum, colon, or pancreas. The diagnosis is usually made by history or problems in these structures.

In summary, the vast majority of back pain problems are benign, and recovery is spontaneous. Surgery in selective cases presents an excellent result. There are many causes for back pain. The correct diagnosis is essential.

One is referred to the classic work of Wiesel, Feffer, Berenstein, and Rothman, from which through the years we have benefited greatly. Their book should be in the library of every physician that sees patients with back pain.

Chapter IX.
The Non-organic Back Examination (Miller)

"Idleness and lack of occupation tend, nay are dragged, towards evil." **Hippocrates** (6, p. 73)

A clear diagnosis has not been established. There are no abnormal physical findings. A complete physical exam has been done. There is no proved diagnosis. Diagnostic tests are not confirmative. The patient still says he is unable to work. **At this stage** an exam by an expert is needed to identify any non-organic physical findings that might be present. After a thorough history, physical examination and diagnostic tests have not revealed a diagnosis one must take the time to do an examination that will **detect non-organic findings**.

We do not use the term **"<u>malingering</u>"** in our report, but we clearly emphasize that the history, examination, and diagnostic tests do not reveal organic disease. We note that the patient has had an extensive examination with consistent non-organic findings. The judge will recognize this, as malingering, which is also fraud. He can rule on the case accordingly without the threat of a personal lawsuit. If the judge asks if this is malingering the answer is, "The negative exam and tests and the presence of non-organic findings make malingering the only reasonable diagnosis."

The examination consists of identifying non-organic:
- "Over-Reactions"
- Non-organic "Back Examinations"
- Non-organic "Neurological Examinations"

The diagnosis of malingering may be a difficult one. It includes excluding pathology that could cause the symptoms and complaints over an unexpected long period of time and is inconsistent with the injury as described. The patient has enjoyed the advantage of having sympathy. The extended sympathy from family, friends, and sometimes his doctor has made him a "slave" to abnormal sensations. The fraudulent mind is not understood. There has been a variable change in moral responsibility. With time malingering produces a gradual mental and moral corruption. There is a loss of work habit, and a stimulus for financial responsibilities is lost. Absence from work demoralizes an individual. One becomes self-centered and even appreciates the benefits of money not earned. They become victims of Workman's Compensation, Social Security Disability, and other government benefits. They learn that they must develop an attitude that exaggerates to maintain pay away from work.

The demoralizing influences noted above places a big responsibility on the doctor to get the patient back to work as soon as possible. The patient is dependent on the doctor. Writing a note declaring a patient unfit for work is easy and usually much appreciated by the patient. I remember a post-operative patient that I gave instructions to begin a walking program and to build up to walking a mile a day. As he was leaving the room he turned and asked if I would give him a disability slip for his car. I told him **his car may be disabled**, but he was not and that he needed to walk.

I remember my wife and I were visiting friends by boat. The marina was almost full and our assigned boat slip was about one fourth mile from the marina restaurant. It was an easy walk. However, after lunch my doctor friend drove us to the boat. He pulled into a disability parking space and placed his disability tag on the rear view mirror. I said to him, "You aren't disabled, where did you get that tag?" He replied, "You are a doctor, aren't you?"

The patient wants the doctor to support him against the government or large company. An adverse report if proved to be wrong can be libel. Medical reports must be given to the patient. Years ago a law was passed that required when one wrote a letter of recommendation for an employee that employee was entitled to have a copy. This was precipitated by politicians who would write a letter for one of their constituents and then write a second letter saying the first one was written for political reasons only. I also remember a chairman of surgery who was asked by one of his residents to write a letter of recommendation. He was told in writing that she wanted a copy, and he was not to send one to anyone else without her express written permission. He wrote the following letter and sent her a copy. "If I stacked all the residents I have ever trained one on top of the other, she would be on the bottom, Sincerely yours." Not many doctors have this kind of courage. Judges and juries frequently do not see the truth in medical evidence. Sympathy may be a big factor with the doctor, judge, and jury. Litigious cases are much more difficult to deal with and find the truth. Many medico-legal cases amount to pitting the wits of the worker and his lawyer against the medical examiner. **The examiner must be completely unbiased and base his opinion only on the medical evidence of his examination and include all the facts.**

The History in the Suspected Non-Organic Patient is always most important in diagnosis.

A.   Non-Organic Over Reactions

1.   Blank Facial Expression
There are no horizontal facial lines as noted in real pain. A blank facial grimace of a malingerer is readily distinguished from a horizontal real painful grimace such as is noted with a patient with ureteral stones. The functional patient has a facial expression that is immediately noted by any experienced physician even though they may not be able to describe it. One must not make an opinion with this alone because the patient may have financial or personal problems that even outweigh his back pain. The attitude of the examiner must be one of compassion and his whole effort should be directed toward helping the patient to recognize his true problem and regain his proper place in society. (Sympathy is different from compassion.

Sympathy is the concept of that which affects one affects the other. An objective approach to a scientific problem eliminates sympathy but not compassion.) One is not to eliminate sympathy in their lives, but only in science. I remember a wonderful lady with five children. Her husband had deserted her. She worked three jobs to support them. She was always cheerful. We all had compassion and sympathy for her. She developed a cancer and was dead in six weeks. She was a great loss to the world and was missed. A malingerer is no loss and not missed as far as the world is concerned. The examiner must stay focused.

2. Verbal- Disproportionate

The patient frequently has a "burning desire" to tell his story. The examiner must not ask leading questions. The history of the injury is frequently repeated and sometimes in slightly different ways. There are frequent new symptoms. He quotes other doctors, nurses, physical therapists, hospital employees, family, friends, and even children. He may avoid good treatment and not show up for an appointment because "he was too sick." (Going to get treatment that he knows he does not need is not worth the effort!) He goes into great details of minor complaints and brings in other medical problems without the whole emphasis being on the back. There may be moaning, hyperventilating, sweating, and over-reactions to local injections. Severe pains and prolonged after-effects are described. The complaints with time become bizarre and unlikely as related to the initial injury.

3. *Exaggerated Muscle Tension*
b. Kamptocormia (Camptocormia)

All the joints and trunk are flexed. The back is flexed forward, the elbows, wrist, and knees are flexed. The arms are frequently abducted. There is no disease process that produces these symptoms.

b. Collapsing

There is poor cooperation on heel and toe walking and at this time the patient sometimes allows the extremities to collapse. He falls slowly or rapidly and incompletely to the floor. This is an obvious fake or non-organic action. I have seen them fall slowly to the floor, but the most characteristic action is catching themselves before they fall all the way. The back can be observed to bend or twist without enduring pain.

c. **Shaking of arms and body**

This is a coarse, irregular, non-physiological, and inconsistent movement.

B. Non-Organic Findings in the Back Exam

1. Questions to answer

- Is the back stiffness real or faked?
- Is the pain real or faked?
- Is there inability to stoop?

Stiffness must be related to rigidity. If one demonstrates there is no rigidity, the stiffness must be faked or imagined. *If the stiffness is faked one must assume the pain is also faked or imagined*.

2. The Specific Non-Organic Back Exam

- **Superficial Tenderness**

Light touch is painful over a wide area. It may be described as tingling or burning. This is non-organic.

- **Diffuse Deep Tenderness**

Palpation painful over a wide area includes all of the lumbar region and extending to the sacral and thoracic region. If one suddenly palpates the neck muscles, this is frequently also described as being tender. (A consistent *localized* tenderness is **not** considered non-organic.)

- **Simulated Fixity (Voluntary Spasm)**

A Lumbar lordosis is normal and is frequently lost with real spasm. If lordosis is present and it is described as being painful to bend forward and lordosis is eliminated and flexion of the spine is noted this is a normal finding and the spine is not fixed. One must test for this.

Have the patient lie on a flat examining table and observe if the lordosis is still present and further observe:
- Flexing of the thighs causes the lordosis to disappear and reveals that the spine is not fixed.
- Lying flat and sitting up also cause the lordosis to go away and may show some flexion.
- Sit in a chair – observe the lordosis while extending the knees and note if the lordosis goes away.

If these maneuvers are not painful as noted with attempted bending, then they are non-organic findings. (The existence of lordois itself virtually rules out an acute back problem and particularly an acute surgical disk. It is said that an exaggerated lordosis protects the back from an acute disk rupture. With an exaggerated lumbar lordosis an **acute** lumbar surgical problem is rare.)

Note a loss of segmentation in the lumbar area. (Keep in mind that the thoracic area plays no or a minimal role in bending. A restriction must be lumbar. The exception I have seen was a young patient age sixteen who had a discitis at T12, and there was diffuse lumbar spasm.)
- Segmentation varies in older people and is frequently lost in the lower lumbar region but retained in the upper lumbar area.

- An acute back strain or an acute lumbar disk frequently causes diffuse spasm and thus loss of all lumbar segmentation. (The pain with an acute strain can be worse than that with an acute herniated disk.)

- The lack of loss of segmentation at least at one level practically rules out a surgical disk. With experience loss of segmentation is usually easily observed even in large patients. In the neutral position note the distance between the posterior lumbar processes. Note this at each level. If they all separate on flexion there is no loss of segmentation. If at one level there is no increase in separation upon flexion, then there is loss of segmentation at that level. If segmentation is present, it essentially rules out acute and probably chronic pathology that is clinically or surgically significant.

3. Simulated tests in the Exam.

Trick or simulation tests to determine if spasm is voluntary (faked) or involuntary (real) are important knowledge for any examiner.

- The number one test, I discovered in 1960 while I was chief of Neurosurgery at the National Naval Medical Center in Bethesda, Maryland. I have taught it hundreds of times since then, but this is the first time it has been published except as a handout. Through these forty-six years I had one neuropsychologist tell me he had heard of the test. After prodding him several times over two years he was never able to provide a source of reference. (I have heard it referred to as the Hunter's Test and the Burn's Test, but I have been unable to find the originating reference.) I discovered this test by accident. I had a patient with a rigid and scoliotic back and classic L4-5 ruptured disk scheduled for surgery the next morning. During my night rounds unknowingly to me someone had asked for an orthopedic consult. When I arrived at the room, my patient was kneeling in a chair, and the orthopedic surgeon was having him move his body. There was no body movement possible when he was standing. The surgeon was testing for hip function. After the orthopedist left, I started over in my exam. While the patient was standing, the back was still completely rigid and without movement. I then had him kneel in a straight chair with the back of the chair to the patient's left side. I placed my foot on his heels to keep him from falling forward and asked him to bend forward as much as he could. He bent over and touched the floor. The back was still rigid. The back has nothing to do with that movement. The value of this maneuver immediately hit me. **A bad back can do it.** When a malingerer is asked to do it, he thinks he is not supposed to be able to do it and refuses. He says it hurts too much. I never ceased to be amazed how quick an honest patient will do this even though he has severe spasm in his back. The difference between the honest and dishonest comes to light. Other features are then recalled such as **tone of voice**, **facial expressions**, the **quickness to do what they are asked**, etc.

- A second test to determine the difference between real and voluntary spasm is as follows. One should always do both tests, but **if a patient has a bad hip, the test above cannot be done.** Have the patient stand. Palpate several times the back muscles. Palpate the muscles on the left side and ask the patient to stand on the left leg. As he maintains his balance the muscles on the left will contract and relax if it is voluntary, and there will be no change if the spasm is real. The process should be repeated on the right side.

- The patient may be bent forward. The flexors of the back are the abdominal muscles, and they may be very tight. Have him lay flat on his back on the table. He is no longer flexed. The abdominal muscles may or may not be soft. Ask him to rise up. If he is unable to assume the same flexed position he had when standing, it is a non-organic finding.

Chapter X.
Non-Organic Findings and The Neurological Exam:

The objective is to identify complaints and abnormalities that are not consistent with the normal anatomy, any disease, or the patient's injury.

A. Motor Weakness
This includes non-anatomic weakness, cogwheel movement of muscles when being tested, giving way (With an honest patient the examiner may overcome a muscle, but only the patient can make it give way.), and poor, slow cooperation.

B. Sensory Abnormalities
These may be non-anatomical such as a "stocking-glove" deficit. Beware of multiple roots and note specifically that the exam is not consistent with a L4, L5, or S1 root or a combination of these.

C. Simulation-Distraction (Trick Tests) with Simple observation
- Note the gait upon entering the office and upon leaving the office when hopefully the examiner will have exhausted the patient's mental capabilities to continue to fake. There is no doubt that in some cases the long exam distracts the patient.
- Place the hat, coat, or clothes hook at the foot of the examining table. Observe the patient as he comes in and stretches, twists, and extends to reach the hook over the foot of the table. (I recently saw this in an Air Force Hospital examining room.) The trick of having the patient put his clothes under the chair was described 89 years ago. (2, p. 244.)

- Have your hand in your pocket, and as you turn toward your desk pull out your hand and drop a coin. Frequently the patient will bend and pick it up.
- Ask the patient to drop his pants and measure his calves. Then turn to your desk and tell him he can dress. (Don't say raise your pants.)
- Ask the patient to dress and in 2-3 minutes return to the room and see the patient lacing his shoes.
- **Axial Loading**

  Place your hand on top of the patient's head and slowly compress the head downward. This does not cause back pain in an honest person. A complaint of back pain with this maneuver is a non-organic finding.
- **Axial Rotation**

  Place hands on both hips behind the patient and rotate the hips and shoulders in the same plane. If this reproduces back pain, it is a non-organic finding.
- **Straight Leg Raising** (SLR)

  This is the most important test for a surgical ruptured disk. If it is negative, surgery at L4-5 or L5-S1 should be questioned. One must learn to properly interpret this test. For it to be positive it must produce sciatic pain. (Pain in hip, posterior thigh, and lateral calf.) The patient is lying flat on the table. Flex the knee and raise it toward the abdomen. If this causes leg pain, it is a non-organic finding. Repeat with the leg extended which is the proper way to do the test. If sciatic pain is present, that is an organic finding. Next, have the patient sit with their back completely against the back of a straight chair. Again bring the already flexed knee upward. This should not produce sciatic pain. Then bring the heel forward to extend the leg, and if sciatic pain is reproduced it is an organic finding. (One must be sure the hips do not slip forward. Sometimes an honest patient will push his hips forward to try and help what you are doing.)

(Recognition is given to **Waddell** who gave a famous report on non-organic signs that subsequently became know as Waddell's signs. I have incorporated most of them in my evaluation of non-organic evaluations. In my experience Waddell's signs alone are suggestive only.)

Chapter XI.
Other Non-Organic Observations

A. Walking Cane:
If one sees a bad back with a walking cane, it is virtually always non-organic. There is no back pain problem without a neurological deficit that a cane can help. Collie in 1917 also noted, "If doctors were less liberal in ordering walking sticks (canes) less treatment would be needed since they fix attention to the patient and promote his exaggeration." (2, p. 381) (In any parking lot or shopping mall one can witness people with walking canes that are out of rhythm with their gait, tipping along, or even being dragged. All this is non-organic or faking.)

B. Back Braces
A back brace is never indicated in a chronic back problem without clear pathology. It creates a dependency and weakens the back. I have seen many patents with a fractured spine that required a cast or brace. They complain profusely about it for a while. However, when it is removed after several weeks they complain even more that they cannot do without it. It has been said that putting a brace on a man for back pain is like a little girl rubbing a turtle's back. When asked why, she said, "Because he likes it." (2, p. 255)

C. Worker Peers and Family
1. One employee told another that if you just tell the doctor you hurt your back and it hurts, the doctor could never tell the difference.
2. Peer workers frequently are helpful. They sometimes know that their co-worker is faking particularly if they have to do

his or her work.

3. Worker peers sometimes tell if the worker is working at another job or at home. The family frequently confirms and has already suspected malingering. ("I don't think there is anything wrong with him.") Some families have gotten tired of the "no work" and many complaints. Input from all individuals who relate to the patient may be revealing.

D. Video Evaluations

Video examiners are frequently hired to video patients' activities when they are not aware of it. The following two stories make two points.

1. One of my partners had a patient he thought was faking pain. He informed the insurance company. They had the patient followed. He was videoed lifting heavy furniture up several flights of stairs and loading and unloading a truck. The patient was shown the video. He said, "That ain't me!" The pathological liar was sent back to work.

2. Thirty-plus years ago I was asked to go to Tampa, Florida to be a court referee examiner. The insurance companies and the patient's examiners gave conflicting medical reports. I am a pilot, and I decided to land at St. Petersburg and spend a day at the beach. The attorneys were going to pick me up, return to Tampa, show me a video, and then we were to drive about forty miles south of Tampa to examine the patient in a clinic/ hospital examining room. The town had a grass runway. I met them there. They showed me the video. The patient was digging in his garden; he was riding a small tractor, and pushing a wheel barrel. I examined him. He had spasm and scoliosis in his back. **There were no non-organic findings**. He had a marked weakness of his quadriceps muscle with over an inch of atrophy. He had a classic L4 nerve root compression that did not show on the studies that were done on him. (This was before the time of the CT and the MRI.) I asked him about the video. He said he went to his garden

one day and tried to dig, but he had to quit after two tries. The next day he rode on his tractor ten feet and had to stop because of leg pain to the middle knee area. The next day he tried to move some plants with a wheel barrel for his wife, but he was unable to do it. **The video had been edited** so that one would suggest continued work. He won his case.

A doctor was a surgical professor in a medical school. A neurologist professor had examined him. After a time he was told there was nothing wrong with his back, and he should return to normal surgical activities. His exam revealed a weak quadriceps and an inch and a half atrophy of the thigh. An x-ray showed a spondylolisthesis of L 3-4. An x-ray had not been done. This is an unusual example of needing an objective test if one does not know how to examine a patient.

Chapter XII.
Summary

A.   Well Known Quotes:

"The most terrifying words in the English language are: I'm from the government and I'm here to help."
Ronald Reagan

"Government's view of the economy could be summed up in a few short phrases: If it moves, tax it. If it keeps moving regulate it. And if it stops moving, **subsidize it.**"
Ronald Reagan

"Ask not what your country can do for you, but what you can do for your country."

John F. Kennedy

After studying Faked Disability for a few years these thoughts are my thoughts:

- Being dependent on undeserved charity or government is an extreme form of slavery. Robbing the government is robbing oneself and their friends.
- A man becomes a thief, he is not born one.
- In the presence of honor, there is not idleness.
- All men have strengths and weaknesses. Some put the weaknesses ahead of the strengths and others the strengths ahead of the weaknesses.

- A calamity in life often exposes virtue or weakness.
- We speak of weakness, but must live strengths or become weak.
- He who walks the right course does not look down, but up.
- Falsely exploiting others always comes to a bad end.
- Faked disability becomes an extreme form of intentional slavery.

Providing help to truly disabled people makes us stronger. Providing support to those faking make all of us weaker.

I thought I had seen it all. No one knows how common the concept of the "Red Badge of Courage" really is. (Desiring an injury so that one can obtain glory in it.) Recently I saw an expensive, handmade sports car convertible with large fenders and lights parked in a large disability-parking place. Hanging from the mirror was a hand made disabled parking sticker. It displayed the usual wheelchair symbol, but this one was bejeweled and with silver reflectors. The large number of people who are proud of being disabled is staggering.

B.   Factors in the Diagnosis of an Abuser:

What is necessary for the diagnosis of a patient with a non-organic syndrome? (**A malingerer**)

1. The History is not consistent with the complaint.
2. The Clinical exam reveals no organic findings related to the complaints. The exam is normal.
3. The diagnostic studies are negative; they do not reveal the pathology to support a diagnosis that explains the patient's pain.
4. The patient has non –organic complaints.
5. The patient has multiple non-organic findings.
6. The motivation for the above may be economic, (The patient does not like his work, and/or enjoys attention), legal, insurance, and if in the military he wants a better assignment or one closer to home, etc. Understanding the individual circumstances frequently supports the diagnosis of the

syndrome. The goals may be recognizable. There may be obvious manipulation or even lying.

7. The physician recognizes and reports the facts.
8. The lawyer does not accept a patient's case who is not disabled as related to the medical facts.

Learning and practicing these techniques will frequently give the physician confidence in his diagnosis of the non-organic syndrome. (Malingering).

The great tragedy of a malingerer is that his life is wasted. His life is "flowing back and forth, errant and ambiguous." (Ovid's, *Metamorphoses*) and he is a "meander." The aimless wandering of a human being. **(21, p. 35)**

Leo Tolstoy (1828-1910), "The more is given the less the people will work for themselves, and the less they work the more their poverty will increase." **(6, p. 543)**

Cicero (106-43B.C.) "The idle mind knows not what it wants." **(6, p. 87)**

EPILOGUE

(A speech addressed to the spectators by an actor at the end of a play.)

Introduction

Epilogue Outline

Introduction
    A.   **Man**
    B.   **Pride**
    C.   **Soul**

Chapter I. Psalm 139: God Places a Great Value On Us and Holds Us in His Hand. (We should Value Ourselves.)

He knew us before we were born, created us, and is with us in all our days that He has planned. We are not to waste our lives. God has placed a great value on us.

Chapter II. Spiritual Gifts From God
    A. Mental Preparation
    B. God Must Have our Attention
    C. How Does One Mentally Prepare
    D. Romans Chapter 12; I Corinthians 12, 13, 14; Acts 2; Revelation 7:10, 11,12, 13, 17.
        1. Romans Chapter 12
        2. I Corinthians 12,13,14
            a. Chapter 12
            b. Chapter 13
            c. Chapter 14
               The "Tongues" Question Answered
    E. Ephesians 4:7-13
    F. Tone of the Ministry with the Holy Spirit
    G. Pentecost Acts 2
    H. Gentiles Included
    I.   "Tongues" Discussion
        1. Acts 2
        2. I Corinthians 13
        3. I Corinthians 14
        4. Other: All are Known Languages

5. Tongues as a Structure in the Mouth

Chapter III. Specific Gifts of the Holy Spirit (Four New Testament References and one Old Testament)
    A. Romans 12: 3-8
    B. I Corinthians Chapters 12-14
        1. Chapter 12
        2. Chapter 13
        3. Chapter 14
    C. Ephesians 4: 7-13
    D. I Peter 4: 10-11 (Instructions to Every Man)
    E. Isaiah 11:2
    F. Miller Lists of Spiritual gifts
    G. Other Biblical References
    H. Discussion of Spiritual Gifts

Chapter IV. The Fruits of the Spiritual Gifts (Galatians 5:22, 23; II Corinthians 3:17,18; Romans 15:13)
    A. Other Moralists List Their Concepts
        1. Gregory the Great
        2. Tertullian
        3. John Cassian
        4. St. Augustine
        5. The Seven Virtues
        6. The Seven Corporal Works of Mercy
        7. The Seven Spiritual Works of Mercy
        8. Benjamin Franklin's 13 Virtues, etc.
        9. The Seven Sages of Greece
        10. The Ten Levels of Love
        11. Henry VIII
    B. John the Baptist
    C. Jesus
    D. The Question that is Demanded: "What is my Gift?"
    E. The Faith That Does Not Do is Dead Faith
    F. The Law

Chapter V. God's Love

VI. Do You Love Me More Than These?
VII. Summary of the Epilogue

Psalm 139: God Holds Us in His Hand.
He will never let us go!

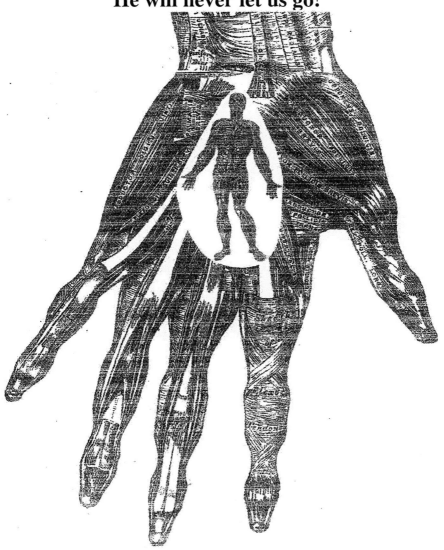

**The human hand is a very complex structure.
We cannot imagine the immense and limitless
"Hand" of God.**

Introduction of the Epilogue:

Problems should not be presented without solutions. Faked disabilities are so widespread in America that a national change in the mentality and morality of America must take place. The change must include all Americans and particularly with physicians and attorneys. The only solution that I can see must come through God's direction for our daily living. This epilogue reveals His directions.

A. Man

Man has been divided by Gnostics into three classes: **(41, p. 528)**
1. The Hylic Man (He never gropes beyond the limitation of matter)
2. The Psychic Man (His intelligent mind originates in the body and perishes with it.)
3. The Pneumatic Man (He rises to the intuitions and perceptions of the soul.)

Every action and occupation "With all diligence should endeavor to be inwardly free and thoroughly master of itself; and that all things be under thee, and not thou under them." **(40, p. 127)**

"If one fails in the highest works, then one should take his stand in works of humility." Humble work will also give one a firm confidence. **(40, p. 147)**

"Patience and humility in adversities are more pleasing to God, than much comfort and devotion when things go well." **(40, p. 159)**

Since men walked with God, there has been an evolution of religion (Miller), but no change in **His** message.

B. Pride:

Pride in ourselves usually proposes much and does little. It shows ecstasy only in public and never in private, which helps the devil. **(41, pp. 546, 547)**

A spiritual man fights spiritual voluptuousness, spiritual sluggishness, spiritual mindlessness, **(41, pp. 551, 559)** and if we lose we return to the man of this world. If we win, our house is a house of peace. **(41, p. 585)** We will continue to occasionally fail and our soul suffers. (We can feel our soul.) (Miller.) God's divine love picks us up, and we return to peace. We repeat this over and over. If one does not know this, they do not understand being close to God. His love guides us through the journey in darkness, and it becomes His light. His secret wisdom for us is like climbing His stairs. The steps are sometimes five degrees and sometimes 100 degrees. At 180 degrees we are going down and must turn around.

C.   Soul

Another view: **(41, pp. 529, 530)** "We discover the Kingdom of God in the center of the soul by the apex of the intellect where our soul and intellect becomes the whole." As man we are sealed in the image of God who gave us an intellect. Man with a soul is raised above all other created things. It transcends all time and place and is in perpetual motion with God as an eternal spring towards life eternal. Our soul was present at the creation of the world and watched the earth formed in all its glory. ***The soul never was because it has always been***. The soul will never end and knows no age, no passage of time, and no limitation in space because it is immortal. **(41, p. 530)** We are left to the conquest of our own souls. We can glorify it, or we can horrify it. **(Miller)** We can with God's help command it or submit to Satan who will command it. We all have a Tree of Life. **(41, p. 533)** We are growing with it or pruning and lapping it off by our sins, instincts, appetites, desires of the body, polluting of our minds, intellect, and sacrificing control of our will when our soul is left without support and falls into eternal darkness.

We can follow the mule paths of life or the rotting bread of our bank accounts to darkness or ride on the spiritual wings of our souls to eternity. We do not need to pray for a Christian's soul, only follow in their footsteps. **(41, p. 539)**

Psalm 139

We search for God.

This Psalm is one of the best-inspired descriptions of some of the attributes of God.

Our minds cannot comprehend all of God.

God's attributes from Psalm 139

Verses 1-6: God as Creator with infinite knowledge, love and awareness of us.

Verses 7-12: God is in all places at all times.

Verses 13-18: God has unlimited authority and power. He is the Almighty.

David's Reverence for God:

Verses 19-24: David Recognizes God as God and himself as God's creation. He asked God to examine him for any wickedness.

To have knowledge of God we must examine and have knowledge ourselves. God's attention to us (He made us) in this Psalm reveals how valuable we are to Him.

PSALM CHAPTER 139

1. O LORD, thou hast searched me, and known *me*.

2. Thou knowest my downsitting and mine uprising, thou understandest my thought afar off.

3. Thou compassest my path and my lying down, and art acquainted *with* all my ways.

4. For *there is* not a word in my tongue, *but*, lo, O LORD, thou knowest it altogether.

5. Thou hast beset me behind and before, and laid thine hand upon me.

6. *Such* knowledge *is* too wonderful for me; it is high, I cannot *attain* unto it.

7. Whither shall I go from thy spirit? or whither shall I flee from thy presence?

8. If I ascend up into heaven, thou *art* there: if I make my bed in hell, behold, thou *art there*.

9. *If* I take the wings of the morning, *and* dwell in the uttermost parts of the sea;

10. Even there shall thy hand lead me, and thy right hand shall hold me.

11. If I say, Surely the darkness shall cover me; even the night shall be light about me.

12. Yea, the darkness hideth not from thee; but the night shineth as the day: the darkness and the light *are* both alike *to thee*.

13. For thou hast possessed my reins: thou hast covered me in my mother's womb.

14. I will praise thee; for I am fearfully *and* wonderfully made: marvellous *are* thy works; and *that* my soul knoweth right well.

15. My substance was not hid from thee, when I was made in secret, *and* curiously wrought in the lowest parts of the earth.

16. Thine eyes did see my substance, yet being unperfect; and in thy book all *my members* were written, *which* in continuance were fashioned, when *as yet there was* none of them.

17. How precious also are thy thoughts unto me, O God! how great is the sum of them!

18. *If* I should count them, they are more in number than the sand: when I awake, I am still with thee.

19. Surely thou wilt slay the wicked, O God: depart from me therefore, ye bloody men.

20. For they speak against thee wickedly, *and* thine enemies take *thy name* in vain.

21. Do not I hate them, O LORD, that hate thee? and am not I grieved with those that rise up against thee?

22. I hate them with perfect hatred: I count them mine enemies.

23. Search me, O God, and know my heart: try me, and know my thoughts:

24. And see if *there be any* wicked way in me, and lead me in the way everlasting.

Chapter I.
God Places a Great Value on Us

Psalm 139: God holds us in his hand wherever we go. He will never let go!

The human hand is a very complex structure. We cannot imagine the immense and limitless "hand" of God. It has complete awareness, understanding and all knowledge that is too wonderful and too big for us.

His hand is in all places at all times.

It has unlimited authority and influence.

It is the hand of **Elohim** in Genesis 1:1 "In the beginning Elohim created." Elohim is repeated 28 times in the first chapter of Genesis. It describes Elohim (God) as the Creator and describes what He did, said, and intended. He glimpsed all animals and all human kind. He created man and gave him an eternal soul. Elohim occurs 2,570 times in the Old Testament and is the descriptive name for God of the Bible. He is the source of and sovereign over all that exists in material and all life in the universe. **Yahweh** is the one personal name for God in the Old Testament. It occurs 5,311 times. It is always spelled with a large capitol L and the small capitals in LORD. Yahweh is the God of Psalm 139. Yahweh is the God of our past, present, and future. He is always with us, intervenes on our behalf, and with Yahweh we will never be alone. In the Exodus Yahweh taught the people that He was the One God "Who is always present." **(53, pp. 18,19, 21, 26, 27)**

Some scholars feel this is the most excellent of all the Psalms of David because it is a devout meditation of God's most complete awareness, knowledge, understanding, and concern for all mankind. We should therefore praise God with our hearts fixed on Him. God created us, knows all about us, and planned our lives with great care. This requires a belief in One God that is not bound by space or time. **(46, p. 402)** Psalm 104 (NIV) elaborates further:

"God stretches out the heavens like a tent, makes the clouds His chariot, rides on the wings of the wind and makes winds His messengers, how many are His works? In wisdom He made them all, and where He opens His hand the world is filled with good things. He looks at the earth and it trembles. But may sinners vanish from the earth and the wicked be no more." We are to praise God as long as we live and pray that out meditations are pleasing to Him.

David is awed that God knows him in such minute detail.

There are wide variations between modern translations in verses 16-20. **(50, p. 402)** One major study of the Old Testament does not mention Psalm 139 **(51, pp. 541-547)** and lists the "royal psalms" as 2, 20, 21, 45, 72, and 110. **(51, p. 563)** One soon gets the impression in a study of the Psalms that the messages therein are so vast that one cannot learn them all in a lifetime. They are as David says filled with knowledge "too high for us."

The doctrine of the knowledge of God is revealed in Psalm 139. God has complete knowledge, awareness, and understanding from the "beginning to the end". He is in all places at all times; He is the Creator. He made us and he knows all about us. He has unlimited authority, influence and is the Almighty over all matter, flesh, and life for all times.

The summary of Psalm 139 reveals the attributes of God's constant attention and protection He gives us and should prompt us to obey Him and see the value He has placed on us. He holds "man" the crowning glory of His creation in His hand. No other god has ever claimed to create and love his creation. Our God stands alone with this attribute noted in Psalm 139.

Charles Spurgeon's (*The Treasury of David*) visions on Psalm 139:
(This section has been selected and abbreviated.) **(55. pp. 258-292)**

"The knowledge and the power of God as Creator with His universal presence will overthrow the powers of wickedness. Psalm 139 is as bright as a sapphire stone or Ezekiel's "terrible crystal." (Ezekiel 1:22) It's light turns night into day. It warns against practical atheism, which denies God and so makes a shipwreck of the soul. **(55, p. 258)** God cannot forget that which He has once known. I may leave God's path, but He will never leave mine. God fills us with awe, so that we sin not; with courage, so that we fear not; with delight, so that we mourn not. Divine knowledge is perfect. God is behind us recording our sins, with us by His grace blotting out the remembrances of them, and before us providing all our wants. We are, whether we like it or not, as near to God as our soul is to our body. His mind is in our mind; Himself within ourselves. His Spirit is over our spirit; our presence is ever in His presence. If we tried to escape God, it would be like flying into the center of the fire to escape the heat. We have the choice of two regions, one of glory and the other of darkness. Foolish men sin in darkness, seen by God because He knows no darkness. We cry with Hagar, "Thou God seest me." (Genesis 16:13) Verse 16 is used by many to support predestination. Spurgeon said, "The large number of words in italics will warn the English reader that it would be unwise to found any doctrine upon the English words; happily there is no temptation to do so." **(55, p. 263)** (I have noted in my previous report that some historians claim Spurgeon was a Calvinist, but his sermons and writings refute this.) God thinks on us who are poor and needy. God thought upon us from old eternity, continues to think upon us every moment, and will think upon us till time shall be no more. Without God man seeks rest on a pillow that is like a razor's edge. If one wants to count the thoughts of God for us, he must go to the beach and count the grains of sand in all the beaches of the world. David said, "If God will not let you live with Him, I will not let you live with me." To blaspheme the name of the Lord is a gratuitous (free) wickedness. This is a mark of the enemies of the LORD. David was an unashamed "hater" because he hated only those who hated good. To love all men with benevolence (a charitable nature) is our duty; but to love any wicked man with complacency (self-satisfaction) would be a crime. **(55, p. 265)** To hate a man for his own sake, or for any evil done to us, would be wrong; but to hate a man because he is the foe of all goodness and the enemy of all righteousness, is nothing more nor less than an obligation. The loyal subject must not be friendly to the traitor."

VERSES 1-6:
God as Creator With Infinite Love and Awareness of Us:

1. O LORD, thou hast searched me, and known *me*.
2. Thou knowest my downsitting and mine uprising, thou understandest my thought afar off.
3. Thou compassest my path and my lying down, and art acquainted *with* all my ways.
4. For *there is* not a word in my tongue, *but*, lo, O LORD, thou knowest it altogether.
5. Thou hast beset me behind and before, and laid thine hand upon me.
6. *Such* knowledge *is* too wonderful for me; it is high, I cannot *attain* unto it.

Verses 1-6 relate the complete, awareness, understanding and knowledge of God.

Verse 1. God's mind had searched, proved, penetrated, pierced, and revealed David as he is. By knowing every detail God knew him intimately. David reflects on the mystery of his own creation and God's gracious preservation of him. He knew how he would look and what would become of him. God's love does not end at Creation.

Verses 2-4 are examples of how well God knew David; He knows every move, every action, when he sits down, when he rises up and even all his thoughts before he has them. ("Afar off" means time not distance). He knows when he walks before he walks. He knows every word (good or bad) before he says it. (Our thoughts are words to God.) **Cicero:** "What men wish or pray in silence, God hears them." **(55, p. 273)** God has David circled, beset, hedged, and in His hand. (God fashioned him last and first.) God's knowledge is too wonderful for him. It is extraordinary - surpassing - too high. (Extraordinary, surpassing, too high are terms used frequently in the Psalms to describe God's wonderful work.) God is not limited by space or time. "O the depth of the riches both of the wisdom and knowledge of God! How unsearchable are his judgments, and his ways past finding out! For who hath known the mind of the Lord? or who hath been his counselor?" (Romans11: 33, 34) (The Egyptians called God the "eye of the world." Thomas Le Blanc, 55, p. 271)

Verse 5: "thine hand" here in Hebrew is "palm of thy hand."

Verse 6: The best discussion of this verse in my study is by Henry Duncan (1774-1846) in **"Sacred Philosophy of Seasons."**(55, p. 273) "His eye at the same instant surveys all the works of His creation, the slightest motion, the smallest insect, the sublimest angels, the meanest, and the most worthless creatures. At the same moment He is listening to praises from grateful hearts in all the world and every thought from the polluted minds of the fallen. An eternity past and an eternity to come are, at the same moment in His eye. His vision is without beginning and without end."

VERSES 7-12: God is in All Places at All times:

7. Whither shall I go from thy spirit? or whither shall I flee from thy presence?
8. If I ascend up into heaven, thou *art* there: if I make my bed in hell, behold, thou *art there.*
9. *If* I take the wings of the morning, *and* dwell in the uttermost parts of the sea; (uttermost parts of the sea means distance. **(49, p. 690)**
10. Even there shall thy hand lead me, and thy right hand shall hold me.
11. If I say, Surely the darkness shall cover me; even the night shall be light about me.
12. Yea, the darkness hideth not from thee; but the night shineth as the day: the darkness and the light *are* both alike *to thee.*

Verses 7-11: God is in all places at all times. We cannot escape the presence of God. "Whither shall I go from thy Spirit?" "…take not thy Holy Spirit from me." (Psalm 51:11)"…thy Spirit is good; lead me into the land of uprightness." (Psalm 143:10) (The heathen asks, "Where is God?" The Christian answers, "Where is He not?")

He is in the heavens above and the depths below. The wings of the morning (speed of Light) and going over the sea God is there. Thy hand leads me and holds me. Darkness is oppressive and cover (sup or shuf) means hide, crush, or bruise. (Same word used in Genesis 3:15 and Job 9:17)

Verses 12: Darkness and light are the same to God. (**Plato:** "God is truth and light His shadow.")

We must see ourselves as open before God. "Can any hide himself in secret places that I shall not see him? saith the LORD. Do not I fill heaven and earth? saith the LORD." (Jeremiah 23:24)

Try to hide and God will be there. The grave does not hide us. (**55, p. 942**) The suicide goes directly to God and His judgment. (Trying to escape from God is like flying into the fire to escape the heat.) (**55, p. 260**) God make us. Parents are only the instruments. God is our chief parent. (**52, p. 942**) God made the universe, the earth and us. He knows us broken down to the smallest cell. He knows our soul.

Plutarch: "Man may not see thee do an impious deed; But God thy very inmost thought can read." (**55, p. 271**)

Over the door of the library of George Seaton Bowes (1884) is, "Innocue vivite, Numen adest." (Live innocently: God is present.") (**55, p. 274**)

Plato knew there was a Deity, "The gods will punish you whether you fly to heaven or depart to Hades, or are carried to a place more wild than these." (**55, p. 274**)

VERSES 13-18:
God Has Unlimited Authority and Power. He is the Almighty:

13. For thou hast possessed my reins: thou hast covered me in my mother's womb.

14. I will praise thee; for I am fearfully *and* wonderfully made: marvellous *are* thy works; and *that* my soul knoweth right well.
15. My substance was not hid from thee, when I was made in secret, *and* curiously wrought in the lowest parts of the earth.
16. Thine eyes did see my substance, yet being unperfect; and in thy book all *my members* were written, *which* in continuance were fashioned, when *as yet there was* none of them.
17. How precious also are thy thoughts unto me, O God! how great is the sum of them!
18. *If* I should count them, they are more in number than the sand: when I awake, I am still with thee.

Verse 13: Covered or created or helped in the womb (created in the womb is also noted in Isaiah 44:24). A better description is in Job 10:11,12. "Thou hast clothed me with skin and flesh, and hast fenced me with bones and sinews. (Tendons for strength) Thou hast granted me life and favour, and thy visitation hath preserved my spirit." God watches over our development in the womb. What a value God has given our soul. He made it after His image, He redeemed it with Christ' blood.

Verse 14: This verse was made famous by Dr. Paul Brand's book titled *"Fearfully and Wonderfully Made."* He also published another famous book, *"The Ten Fingers of God."* Dr. Brand is world-renowned and the pioneer of reconstructive surgery of the hands. He developed the techniques in India while operating and reconstructing the hands of lepers. This verse reveals clearly that David was very mindful of God's marvelous creation of human beings. David praises God and gives thanks to Him. Substance is frame or skeleton, which is made in secret but is not hidden from God. (When I read the pollution of this verse by one of the modern translators I was inspired to study verse 14 and then on to the entire Psalm.)
Verse 15: Substance was "my strength" or "my bones." (45, p. 781)
Verse 16: Substance that is imperfect or unformed is the embryo. My member (body) was designed before it came about and includes the number of days he will live. (Some think this refers to everyday

activities and not days of his life.) "Thy book" here is God's mind. (**49, p. 690**) Another author (**54**) transposes two Hebrew letters so that the term "embryo" is changed to "deeds." I always enjoy the mental aberrations of translators who change words written 2000 plus years ago and after hundreds of translators have done it before them. This one is particularly interesting since he admits he does not know Hebrew. I am with Spurgeon who said he lost faith in modern translators. (**55, p. 258**)

Verse 17: God's thoughts of him are precious, great, and innumerable. "For I know the plans I have for you," declares the LORD, "plans to prosper you and not to harm you, plans to give you hope and a future." (Jeremiah 29:11, NIV) Our thoughts of God must be above all other thoughts. God's care does not end in creation. (**47, p. 474**)

Verse 18: When he awakes each day God is still with him and extending His plans for him. God's thoughts for him outnumber the sand. The infinite mind of God is compared to the limited mind of man and especially as it related to man. (Rules out evolution) God's people are precious to God. A Christian has a great advantage over other men in this verse. A Christian lies down with God. He falls asleep in God's arms, like a child in his mother arms. He is lulled to sleep with the love and hope of God. He knows he will find it with Him when he wakes. God winds up the Christian's heart for the day. (**55, p. 263**)

Verses 19-24:
David recognizes God as God and himself as God's Creation. He asked God to examine him for any wickedness. (Our relationship to the wicked is discussed.)

19. Surely thou wilt slay the wicked, O God: depart from me therefore, ye bloody men.
20. For they speak against thee wickedly, *and* thine enemies take *thy name* in vain.
21. Do not I hate them, O LORD, that hate thee? and am not I grieved with those that rise up against thee?
22. I hate them with perfect hatred: I count them mine enemies.
23. Search me, O God, and know my heart: try me, and know my thoughts:

24. And see if *there be any* wicked way in me, and lead me in the way everlasting.

God's Righteous Judgment:

Verse 19: David asked God to slay the wicked, bloody men, (The doctrine known as the end of sinners.) who are also God's enemies. "Let your sharp arrows pierce the hearts of the king's enemies; let the nations fall beneath your feet." (Psalm 45:5, NIV) David also refers to sinners as blood men in Psalm 26:9)

Verse 20: They use God's name for evil purposes. The wicked are open to God. "... the Lord is coming... to judge everyone, and to convict all the ungodly of all the ungodly acts they have done in the ungodly way, and of all the harsh words ungodly sinners have spoken against Him." (Jude 14, 15) God loves the sinner, but hates the sin. **(48, p. 282)**

Verse 21: David would have nothing to do with God's enemies. (*"Hate"* here means, *"reject"* and is not associated with the Hebrew words of love and hate. It is not emotional, but a choice one over the other.) **(44, p. 892)**

Verse 22: Perfect hatred: (This reminds one of German chancellor Otto von Bismark's (1815-1898) speech to his enemies. "It is the fear of God which makes us love peace and keep it. He who breaks it against us ruthlessly will learn the meaning of 'warlike love.'" He was a strong Protestant and anti-Catholic. (*The World's Greatest Speeches*, Copeland, Lamm, McKenna, Dover Publishers, Inc., 1942-1999, p. 123.) Sin is hated; sinners are lamented by all that fear God. "The deeds of faithless men I hate; they will not cling to me. Men of perverse heart shall be far from me; I will have nothing to do with evil." (Psalm 101:4) "Augustine describes the perfect hatred as such perfection that he hated the iniquity for which men were punished as he loved the manhood for which he prayed."**(55, p. 286)** Another view is from William Arnot (1875). It is a matter of ones orientation. The non-believer "cherishes his sins against a dreaded God." The Christian takes part with a "reconciled God against His hated sins." **(55, p. 287)** We love the enemy, but don't entertain them. (We hate their actions.)

Verse 23: Search (Test) me and show me I am not wicked. To have knowledge of God we must examine and have knowledge of ourselves. (David also asked God to examine him in Psalm 26:2.)

Verse 24: Any wicked way (anxious thoughts, or anxiety, in NIV) a good man desires to know the worst of himself and asks God to root it out of him. God comforts our anxiety. "In the multitude of my thoughts within me thy comforts delight my soul." (Psalm 94:19) (**Plato**: "The life which is unexamined is not worth living.") I like an old quote, "The young hypocrite tries to appear more vicious than he really is. The old hypocrite tries to appear more virtuous than he really is." (Reference unknown) How beautiful is the humility of David.

Everlasting probably means prolonged life as he followed the LORD or a desire for and expectation of eternal life. **(44, p. 893)**

Are we to hate our enemies? A reference to review is a reference from the martyrs: "And they cried with a loud voice, saying, How long, O Lord, holy and true, dost thou not judge and avenge our blood on them that dwell on the earth?" They were told to "wait a little longer until others were killed." (Revelation 6: 10,11)

A word to Babylon from their captives: "Happy is he who repays you for what you have done to us." (Psalm 137: 8 NIV) "Blessed shall he be who shall seize and 'dash' thine infants against the rock." (Psalm 137:9, The Septuagint) Jesus said, **"They will dash you to the ground, you and the children within your walls...."** (Luke 19:44) It is amazing that these are the only two places in the whole Bible where this verb for "dash" is used. (By David in Psalm 137:9 [Septuagint] and by Christ in Luke 19:44.)

These are not just prayers for vengeance, but are earnest prayers and pleadings to God. These are passionate requests for God and

His glory against those who boast against God. The deeper sense message here is for those who are in the presence of evil and they pay no attention to it. A prayer against evil seems permitted as long as it is not a personal vendetta, but is for God's glory.

Psalms 2-8 comes to mind with these scriptures:

Psalm 2: "Why do the heathen rage... take counsel against the LORD... speak unto them in His wrath, break them with a rod of iron... dash them in pieces."

Psalm 3: "...they increased trouble for me... thou hast smitten all mine enemies upon the cheek bone; and hast broken the teeth of the ungodly."

Psalm 4: "...How long will ye turn my glory into shame?"

Psalm 5: "...the foolish shall not stand...thou *hatest* all workers of iniquity, thou shalt *destroy* them and abhor the bloody and deceitful man,... their inward part is very wickedness; their throat is an open sepulcher; they flatter with their tongue....Destroy thou them, O God."

Psalm 6: "Let mine enemies be ashamed and sore vexed."

Psalm 7: "...in thine anger, lift up thyself because of the rage of mine enemies: and awake for me to the judgment that thou hast commanded. My defense is of God... God is angry with the wicked every day....He hath also prepared for them the instruments of death, their mischief shall return upon his own head..."

Pslam 8: "...Because of thine enemies, that thou mightest still the enemy and the avenger."

The famous question: "What is man that thou art mindful of him?"

David said he hated those who hated God, "...who rise up against God." (Psalm 139:21,22, NIV) These words of hatred need further collaboration in the scriptures.

David says in Psalm 69 that those who hate him "outnumber the hairs of his head". (Verse 4) "The insults of God falls on him." (Verse 9) May the table set before them become a snare; may it become retribution and a trap. (Verse 22) He petitions God to, "Give them wrath, anger (Verse 24), may they be deserted and with no one in their tents, (Verse 25), do not let them share in your salvation, (Verse 27), blot them out of the book of life, and not be listed with the righteous. (Verse 28)

David continues in Psalm 109 and says to God, appoint an evil man to oppose this enemy, (verse 6), let him be tried and found guilty and let his prayers condemn him, (verse 7), let his days be few (verse 8) , may his children be fatherless and his wife a widow (verse 9), his children be beggars and driven from ruined home (verse 10) , may no one be kind or take pity on their children, (verse 12), and may their sin always remain before the LORD (verse 15). (**Plato:** "The only escape from evil is becoming holy.")

The people were also required to say "Amen" to the curses of the people as noted in Deuteronomy 27: 15-26.

The deeper sense meaning is to hate evil and not be associated with it and know that God will deal with them in a way that will be horrible to them.

The way of godliness is everlasting, true, good, and profitable and all believers in God desire this and never tire of it. We love to go to church all the time.

Plato: "Atheism is a disease of the soul before it becomes an error of understanding."

Job 32:8 "But there is a spirit in man: and the inspiration of the Almighty giveth them understanding."

Chapter II.
Our Spiritual Gifts from God administered through the Holy Spirit:

Spiritual Gifts are given to us that we may be established.

"For I long to see you, that I may impart unto you some spiritual gift, to the end ye may be established." (Romans 1:11)

"That we henceforth be no more children, tossed to and fro, and carried about with every wind of doctrine, by the sleight of men, and cunning craftiness, whereby they lie in wait to deceive." (Ephesians 4:14)

Jesus said we should judge some things for ourselves. **"Yea, and why even of yourselves judge ye not what is right?"** (Luke 12:57)
He is saying you yourselves should know what is right.

(Do not read this unless you are physically excited and mentally relaxed. You will not understand it if you are physically tired, mentally tense, or stressed.)

A. Mental Preparation
One cannot jump into the scriptures on spiritual gifts. One cannot learn spiritual gifts while daydreaming or drinking coffee and eating cake. One cannot do as a physician does when he looks up the correct dose for an antibiotic. (There may be one similarity here since the physician must also review any adverse effects of the drug

and the effects if he gives the wrong drug to a particular patient.) The teacher of spiritual gifts must be older, experienced in life, fully academically trained, and with proven spiritual qualities. Spiritual gifts cannot be taught in a thirty-minute Sunday School lesson or a one-hour lecture after dinner.

B. God Must Have Our Attention
Spiritual gifts cannot be understood by a non-believer or even a new Christian. Only after God "burned the lips of Isaiah and purged him of his sins" was he able to hear the voice of the Lord. (Isaiah 6:6-8). There is no doubt that God sometimes gets our attention in "foxholes", terminal illness, and other tragedies. I remember a personal doctor friend who had everything except eternal salvation. He was raised with a "silver spoon in his mouth". He had cancer and was operated. There was no change. The cancer recurred, all treatment failed, the end was near, and he died. I received a letter from another friend of ours who was a dedicated, shameless Christian, and soul winner. He with happy tears informed me that our friend had accepted Christ and died a sincere Christian. The brief time this man was a Christian has become a proof testimony to many people.

C. How does one mentally prepare for a scriptural study of the gifts offered by the Holy Spirit?
Is it by prayer and scripture or scripture and prayer? Sometimes prayer helps me get into the scriptures and other times the scripture helps me get into prayer. Nevertheless it requires both. There is a mental preparation required. God must have our attention.

D. Romans Chapter 12; I Corinthians 12, 13, 14; Acts 2; Revelation 7, 10, 11,12, 13, 17. (Four scriptural references for Spiritual Gifts.)

1. Romans Chapter 12 (Read all of Romans Chapter 12.)
Romans 12
1. I beseech you therefore, brethren, by the mercies of God, that ye present your bodies a living sacrifice, *holy*, *acceptable* unto God, which is your reasonable service.

2. And be not conformed to this world: but be ye transformed by the *renewing of your mind*, that ye may prove what is that good, and acceptable, and perfect, will of God.

3. For I say, through the grace given unto me, to every man that is among you, not to think of himself more highly than he ought to think; but to think soberly, according as God hath dealt *to every man* the measure of faith.

4. For as we have many members in one body, and all members have not the same office:

5. So we, being many, are one body in Christ, and *every one members one of another.*

6. Having then gifts differing according to the grace that is given to us, whether prophecy, let us prophesy according to the proportion of faith;

7. Or ministry, let us wait on our ministering: or he that teacheth, on teaching;

8. Or he that exhorteth, on exhortation: he that giveth, let him do it with simplicity; he that ruleth, with diligence; he that sheweth mercy, with cheerfulness.

9. Let love be without dissimulation. Abhor that which is evil; cleave to that which is good.

10. Be kindly affectioned one to another with brotherly love; *in honour preferring one another*;

11. **Not slothful in business;** fervent in spirit; serving the Lord;

12. Rejoicing in hope; patient in tribulation; *continuing instant in prayer*;

13. Distributing to the necessity of saints; given to hospitality.

14. Bless them which persecute you: bless, and curse not.

15. Rejoice with them that do rejoice, and weep with them that weep.

16. Be of the same mind one toward another. Mind not high things, but condescend to men of low estate. Be not wise in your own conceits.

17. Recompense to no man evil for evil. Provide things honest in the sight of all men.

18. If it be possible, as much as lieth in you, live peaceably with all men.

19. Dearly beloved, avenge not yourselves, but rather give place unto wrath: for it is written, Vengeance is mine; I will repay, saith the Lord.

20. Therefore if thine enemy hunger, feed him; if he thirst, give him drink: for in so doing thou shalt heap coals of fire on his head.

21. **Be not overcome of evil, but overcome evil with good**.

Romans 13:1

1. Let every soul be **subject unto the higher powers**. For there is no power but of God: the powers that be are ordained of God.

Notes:

- We must be holy acceptable to God. v.1
- We must be transformed by the renewing of our minds. v.2
- We must think soberly and measure our faith. v.3
- We are all one body in Christ, everyone members of one another. (v.5)
- Our gifts are according to God's grace. (v.6)
- What we do, do with simplicity, rule with diligence, show mercy with cheerfulness (v.8), love without false appearance, hate that which is evil, cleave to good (v.9), be kind, have brotherly love, in honor prefer one another (v.10), do good in business, dedicated in spirit, serve the Lord (v. 11), rejoice in hope, patient in problems, continue in prayer (v.12), give and support our pastors, be hospitable (v. 13), bless them that wrong you, do not curse (v.14), rejoice and weep with your brothers (v.15), be of the same mind not as high things, but condescend to men of low estate, be not wise in your own conceits (v.16), do not return evil for evil, be honest in all things (v.17), if possible live peaceably (v. 18), vengeance is the Lord's (v.19), feed and give drink to your enemy (v.20), and remember there is no power, but of God. (13:1)

The specific gifts noted in Romans 12 are in verses six and seven. They include: *prophesy, ministry, teaching, exhortation, giving, leadership, and mercy.* (Prophesy in the New Testament does not mean predicting the future as in the Old Testament, but means telling the true word of God. In other words, one must educate themselves from the scriptures **and** listen to God to do this.)

2. I Corinthians Chapters 12, 13, 14:

Read I Corinthians Chapter 12, 13, 14
a. I Corinthians Chapter 12
Paul says, "Now concerning spiritual gifts, brethren, I would not
    have you ignorant." (12:1) Chapter 12 gives God's rules for
    spiritual gifts. They are only given to Christians. (v.1-3) (Those
    who confess Christ as Savior.) All gifts come from God. (v.
    4-6) Each Christian has at least one gift. (v.17) The gifts are to
    benefit all in the church. (v.7) There is diversity in unity. (v.8-
    10) Gifts are given as the Spirit wills. (v.11) All the gifts are
    necessary for the church. (v.14-26) There is a listing of the gifts
    chronologically. (v. 27-28) Every gift is not available to every
    Christian. (v. 29-30) One may desire and seek certain gifts (v.
    12:31; 14:1), but as noted in verse eleven the gifts are given as
    the Spirit wills.

b. I Corinthians Chapter 13.
All spiritual gifts are worthless without love. As noted in
    verses 1-3, *tongues, prophesy, knowledge, faith*, and
    giving are worthless without love. Verses 4-7 reveal certain
    characteristics of love that come from God including; long
    suffering, no envy, does not push self, is not conceited, has
    good behavior, does not seek for self, is patient, thinks no evil,
    does not love sin, but loves truth, and bears, believes, hopes,
    and endures all things. Verses 8-12 reveal that all these gifts go
    away when Jesus returns. (They are all temporary.) Verse 13
    reveals that the greatest of gifts is **love**.

c. I Corinthians Chapter 14. (The "Tongues" Question
    Answered)

This chapter defines what is meant by "tongues" in the scriptures and reveals certain criteria for the validity of the understanding of the "tongue" question. Note the singular (tongue) and plural (tongues).

The singular is described by the original King James Version translators as an "unknown " tongue. The singular tongue is *pagan gibberish and useless*. It is not from the Holy Spirit. In all the English and Greek languages *there is no listing of (unknown) languages*. If it is unknown it is unintelligible and to try and understand it causes confusion. God is not a God of confusion. (I Corinthians 14:33). To claim to speak in an *"unknown" tongue is an insult to God and the Holy Spirit* and *thus is heresy* for sure (Doctrine contrary to God's word) and I believe it is also **blasphemy**. (Lack of reverence for God and His sacred word.) This pagan gibberish (Unknown tongue) is noted in Chapter 14: 2, 4, 13, 14, 19, and 27).

The plural (tongues) in the scripture refers to knowledge of known languages. It is noted in verses 14: 6, 18, 22, 23, and 29).

Paul in his day at the church in Corinth, just as we do today, had people that did not understand his teachings. They continued to be a problem; therefore, he established certain rules for those *who spoke gibberish*. He told them they were trying to glorify themselves and not the church. (14:4) "Ye speak into the air." (14:9) He said you are a barbarian". (They did not understand the barbarian languages.) Paul also noted something that is still modern. People were saying "Amen" to things they did not understand. (14:16) Paul goes on to say the *gibbering is harmful to the unbelievers* because when they hear it they think you are mad. (14:22,23) (I must admit that when I visited a large mental hospital several years ago I heard similar voices. One whole room of patients there though they were Jesus. They would not speak to each other as each one thought the other was a fake.)

Paul's rules for speaking in tongues required that only two or three be present and *one must interpret* what is said. (14:27) **If no one can interpret your gibbering,** then **"shut up,"** get by yourself, and speak only to God. (14:28) The last part of this verse could support a "private prayer language", but is still between the person and God. *If one makes it public, it is gibberish or pagan.*

The very title of the Tongues Question denotes a lack of understanding. *The primary issue is not tongues, but the Holy Spirit.*

The scriptural references to being filled with the Holy Sprit:
As we review these references keep in mind that *unless one has been "filled" with the Holy Spirit they are not saved.*

E. Ephesians 4:7-13.
Here one notes some overlapping with other scriptures concerning spiritual gifts. "But unto **every one of us** is given grace according to the measure of the gift of Christ." (4:7) Verses 8-10 describes Christ as descending and ascending to fulfill all things. (Verse 8 is quoting Psalm 68:18)

Verse 11 describes gifts to apostles, prophets, evangelists, pastors, and teachers. (This is also quoted in the *Didache*, *The Teachings of the Apostles*.) Verse 12 describes the purpose, as the perfecting of the saints for the work of the ministry, and the edifying of the body of Christ. (The Church) Verse 13 describes us in "the unity of the faith, with knowledge of the Son of God, unto our perfection, unto the measure of the fullness of Christ."

F. The Tone of the Ministry with the Holy Spirit is set by I Peter 4:10-11.
 "As every man hath received the gift, even so minister the same one to another, as good stewards of the manifold grace of God. If any man speak, let him speak as the oracles of God; if any man minister, let him do it as of the ability which God giveth: that God in all things may be glorified through Jesus Christ, to whom be praise and dominion for ever and ever. Amen."

The tone for the elders is established in I Peter 5:1-4. "Take oversight willingly and without restraint and 'feed' the flock of God. (v. 2) Do not be as lords, but as examples. (v. 3) And receive a crown of glory when the chief shepherd appears." (v. 4)

The scripture continues with advice to young people, "Submit yourselves to the elder. Yea, all of you be humble, not proud, and give grace to the humble and God will exalt you in due time." (I Peter 5: 5-6)

G. Acts 2: Pentecost

The most visible reference of the Holy Spirit being given to us in the Bible is the description of the day of Pentecost. One must read all of Acts Chapter 2. (Some manuscripts entitle it as the "Acts of the Apostles.") It also may be called the "Acts of the Holy Spirit through the Apostles."

"And when the day of Pentecost was fully come, they were all with one accord in one place." (Acts 2:1) "There was the sound of a mighty wind…cloven tongues like as of fire, …and they were all filled with the Holy Spirit, and began to speak with other tongues." (Languages) (Acts 2:2-4) People from all languages and from all over the world *understood each other*. (Acts 2:4-11) This was another one of God's miracles. They were all witnesses that they had received God's promise of the Holy Spirit. (Acts 2: 32, 33) Paul preached, "Repent, and be baptized every one of you in the name of Jesus Christ for ('because of') the remission of sins, and ye shall receive the gift of the Holy Spirit." (Acts 2:38) About three thousand souls were saved. (Acts 2:31) There were many other "wonders and signs" done by the apostles. (Acts 2:43)

At this point one must clearly understand the difference between being baptized with the Holy Spirit and baptism with water. They are entirely different events.

There is only one scripture in the entire Bible that defines baptism by the Spirit. (I Corinthians 12:13), " For by one Spirit are we all baptized into one body, whether we be Jews or Gentiles, whether we be bond or free; and have been all made to drink into one Spirit." The word *"baptize"* means to *"immerse"* or a better understanding is to be *"plunged into."* The person baptized is plunged into the thing he is baptized in. When we are baptized by water we are immersed or plunged into water. Now, get this, we are not plunged into the Holy Spirit. The Holy Spirit is "plunged into us." "And they were filled with the Holy Spirit at Pentecost." Acts 2:4; 4:31; 9:17; 13:9. And the Holy Spirit "came upon them." Acts 19:6 Jesus said, **"But ye shall receive power, after that the Holy Ghost is come upon you."** (Acts 1:8)

The scriptures make it clear that being baptized by the Holy Spirit means that the Holy Spirit is "plunged" into us and we are not "plunged" or "immersed" into the Holy Spirit. **The receiving of the Holy Spirit is the baptism with the Holy Spirit.**

H.   Gentiles Included
The Jews themselves at the house of Cornelius were "astonished, as many as came with Peter, because that on the Gentiles also was poured out the gift of the Holy Spirit." (Acts 10:45) This is described again. "And as I began to speak, the Holy Ghost fell on them, as on us at the beginning. Then remembered I the word of the Lord, how that He said, **John indeed baptized with water; but ye shall be baptized with the Holy Ghost."** (Acts 11:15,16)

Other examples of believers becoming filled with the Holy Spirit is noted in Acts 4:31; 9:17; 10:45; 13:9; 19:6. In 10: 46 they spoke in tongues (languages) that were understood because God was magnified. (This was in the house of Cornelius). In 19: 6 they spoke in tongues that were understood and prophesied. (This means they spoke with the truths of God and does not refer to predicting the future.)

And finally the famous, "Then Peter said unto them, Repent, and be baptized every one of you in the name of Jesus Christ 'because' of the remission of sins, and ye shall receive the gift of the Holy Spirit." (Acts 2:38) Note the word "for" is better translated "because" as noted by **Herschel Hobbs** and others. There was added the same day about 3,000 souls. (Acts 2:41) One must clearly understand the meaning of being baptized by the Holy Spirit before one can understand the meaning of tongues in the Bible. Christ is the baptizer and immerses or plunges the Holy Spirit into believers. We are all baptized into one body. (I Corinthians 12: 13) The body has many members. (I Corinthians 12:12,14) We are also baptized in the body of Jesus Christ by the Holy Spirit. (Romans 6:33) There are no believers (Christians) who have not received the Holy Spirit. *This can only be a one-time event or otherwise the body of Christ would be distorted.* "There is one body, and one Spirit..."(Ephesians 4:4) The church, the body of Christ, is composed of every believer since Pentecost. Christ's salvation is perfect. *There is no need and there is no reference anywhere in the Bible for a second baptism, of the Holy Spirit*. One time does it all. If a person is looking for the Holy Spirit and has not been baptized by the Holy Spirit they are not a Christian. We are "born again" when the Holy Spirit enters us. There is no sense in those who think they must be *"born over and over again"* and keep the Holy Spirit "coming and going" from our saved souls. Such a perceived need shows an *ignorance of the word of God.* (There are reports of people being "saved" many times usually going from church to church. One individual was described as being "saved" fourteen times. Such people are all fakes and ignorant of the scriptures.)

I. The Tongues Question Discussed:

1. **Acts 2:** I count nine times where the word "tongue" or "tongues" is used in the book of Acts. (2:3,4,8,11,26) (five times in Chapter 2), and 4:31; 10:46; 13:9; 19:6.

Acts 2:3 Tongues like fire of the Holy Spirit

Acts 2:4, 8, 11 This represents another miracle where every nation under heaven has understanding with each other. Tongue and tongues here represents languages of many nations. Language represented also in 1:19; 21:40; 22:2; 26:14.

Acts 2:26 "My tongue was glad." This is a quote of David from Psalm 16:9. "Therefore my heart is glad, and my glory rejoiceth: my flesh also shall rest in hope." Tongue here means David's speech, knowledge, or glory was glad.

Acts 4:3, 8, 31; 6:3,7; 7:51, 55. The word tongue is not used, but it reveals "those filled with the Holy Spirit had the power to *speak the word of God with boldness*."

Acts 10: 44,45,46 Peter spoke to Jews and Gentiles and the Holy Spirit fell on them and *"they spoke with tongues magnifying God"*. They received knowledge and power that exalted God. They understood what was said.

Acts 19:6 "…the Holy Spirit came on them; and they spake with tongues, and prophesied." This was language **all the different men understood**. (Prophesy in the scriptures before the Middle Ages meant proclaiming what was already written word.) (**p. 1953**, MacArthur)

2. **I Corinthians 13**
    13:1 speaking in a known **language**
    13:8 language fails, but not love.

3. **I Corinthians 14**
    a. When "tongues" is plural it is a language as noted in 14:5, 6,18, 21, 22, 23, 29,and 39.

    b. When tongue is singular it is an **unknown tongue** or just gibberish (confused speech). There is no listing of unintelligible speech. It is just gibberish, but King James is kind and calls it an unknown tongue. It is also pagan and is noted in 14: 2, 4, 9, 13, 14, 19, 26, and 27.

    c. **14:28** "But if there be no interpreter, let him keep silence in the church; and let him speak to himself,

117

and to God." In the context of this verse it probably refers to *pagan gibberish.* However, since the problem of "private prayer language" has been exposed in the Southern Baptist Convention this needs to be discussed. I have heard people pray in church in English particularly with repetitive phrases that I did not understand. It was gibberish to me, but may have had meaning to God. The term "private prayer language" is a poor, non-descriptive term, if it is not in English. (Where English is the language.) If it is purposely *so rapidly repetitive* that one cannot understand it, it must be considered pagan gibberish. Because of the lack of a clarified description the term as publicized is meaningless. (This is different than "speaking in tongues.")

4. Other: All are known languages

Revelation 14:6 "And I saw another angel fly in the midst of heaven, having the everlasting gospel to preach unto them that dwell on the earth, and to every nation, and kindred, and tongue, and people."

I Corinthians 12:10, 28	Languages
Revelation 7:9	Languages
10:11	Languages
11:9	Languages
13:7	Languages
17:15	Languages

5. Where the terms "tongue" and "tongues" is noted, as in the *tongue structure* in the mouth, it is not relevant to our subject. (Such as "gnawing the tongue".) The 19 references not relevant include:

Mark 7:33; 7:35, Luke 1:64; 16:24, John 5:2, Romans 3:13; 14:11, Philippians 2:11, James 1:26; 3:4; 3:6; 3:8, I Peter 3:10, I John 3:18, Revelation 5:9; 9:11; 14:6; 16:10,16.

Chapter III.
Specific Gifts of the Holy Spirit

(*Four New Testament References:* Romans 12:3-8; I Corinthians Chapters 12-14; Ephesians 4:7-13; I Peter 4: 10-11) and *One Old Testament Reference*) (*Isaiah 11:2*)

A.   Romans 12:3-8

- Prophesy (Knowing and giving God's teaching) (verse 6)
- Ministry (Serving) (verse 7
- Teaching (verse 7)
- Exhortation (Encouraging) (verse 8)
- Giving (verse 8)
- Leadership (verse 8)
- Mercy (verse 8)

B.   I Corinthians Chapters 12 - 14

1. Chapter 12 (gives the fullest list of Spiritual Gifts)
- All men are given a gift by the Holy Spirit to benefit all men. (verse 7)
- Message of wisdom (verse 8)
- Message of knowledge (verse 8)
- Faith (verse 9)
- Healing (verse 9)
- Miraculous powers (verse 10)
- Prophesy (verse 10)
- Distinguishing between spirits (verse 10)

- Speaking in different kinds of tongues (languages) (verse 10)
- Interpretation of tongues (verse 10)
  God ranks Gifts (verse 28) (This is chronological and is not listed as to which is the most important.)
- Apostles
- Prophets
- Teachers
- Wonders of miracles
- Healing
- Help others
- Administration
- Speaking different languages

2. **Chapter 13**
- Love
- Tongues (verse 1)
- Prophesy (verse 2)
- Knowledge (verse 3)
- Faith (verse 2)
- Giving (verse 3)

3. **Chapter 14**
- Love
- Prophesy (verse 1, 3, 4, 5, 6, 22, 24, 31, 39) to:
  1. Edification, instruction, teach
  2. Exhortation, encourage
  3. Comfort
- Unknown tongue (verse 2, 4, 13, 14, 18, 27)
- Tongues – Languages (verse 6,18, 22, 23, 29)

C. **Ephesians 4: 7-13**
- Grace (verse 7)
- Apostles (verse 11)
- Prophets (verse 11)
- Evangelists (verse 11)
- Pastors (verse 11)

- Teachers (verse11)

D.   I Peter 4: 10-11 Instructions to Every Man
- Divine grace (verse 10)
- Minister to one another as good stewards (verse 10)
- Speak with a divinely inspired message (verse 11) (Prophecy)
- Minister to the best of his ability (verse 11)

E.   Isaiah 11:2
Isaiah 11:2 lists seven gifts of the Holy Spirit: "And the Spirit of the LORD shall rest upon Him".

1. The Spirit of Wisdom
2. and understanding
3. of counsel
4. and might(Power, fortitude)
5. the Spirit of knowledge
6. piety (godliness) This is left out of some translations,   but it is in the original **Septuagint.**
7.ˋ and the fear of the LORD

Ephesians 2:20
The foundation of God's people is built upon the apostles and prophets and Jesus Christ is the chief cornerstone. "The holy city, New Jerusalem, coming from God, Revelation 21:2 and the wall of the city had twelve foundations, and in them the names of the twelve aportles of the Lamp." (Revelation 21:14)

F. The Sixteen Miller Listings of the Spiritual Gifts
(Because of overlapping and the difference in certain synonyms in various translations such a list may differ from person to person.)

- Prophecy (Speaking with a divinely inspired message)
- Apostles, **Ministry, Evangelists, Pastors** (Serving)
- Teaching
- Exhortation (encouraging)
- Giving, **helping others, stewardship**

- Leadership, **Administration**
- Mercy
- Wisdom
- Knowledge
- Faith
- Healing
- Miraculous powers
- Distinguishing between spirits
- Speaking in different kinds of tongue (languages)
- Interpretation of tongues
- Grace

Counting those under-lined, as separate entities would make the number of Spiritual Gifts twenty-two instead of sixteen. If one adds love and salvation (being "born again") as a spiritual gift the number becomes twenty-four. The noted references clearly give the above as spiritual gifts. One cannot number the many blessings from God, which might be considered Spiritual Gifts. Lists such as the ones above are probably only valuable academically. (Such as when teaching the subject.) If one claims such a gift or even a gift not listed, it is between him or her and God since it cannot be proved whether true or false.

G. Discussion of Spiritual Gifts, Romans 8: 9, 16
A Christian can recognize another Christian by the witness of the Holy Spirit in him!

"But ye are not in the flesh, but in the Spirit, if so be that the Spirit of God dwell in you. Now if any man have not the Spirit of Christ, he is none of His."

"The Spirit itself beareth **witness** with our spirit, that we are the children of God."

"Spiritual Gift"
- **Pneumatikon** in Greek: – a thing, event, or individual that serves as an instrument of the Spirit.

- **Charisma**: (related to the word *"charis"* which means grace or favor.) an event word or action, which is a firm expression of grace or serves as a means of grace.
- **Ton pneumatikon:** Paul used this synonymously with Charisma, which is literally the "spiritual things." It describes an endowment of spiritual gifts given by the Lord to various individuals in the church. A spiritual gift is an "act of God's Spirit" denoting God's grace in word or deed, which benefits others.

H. Other Biblical References
- Every man his proper gift of God (I Corinthians 7:7)
- Paul imparts spiritual gifts by the Holy Spirit in him. (Romans 1:11)
- Free gift by the grace of God is *Jesus Christ* and by Him grace abounds to many. (Romans 5:15)
- Through Him we receive the abundance of grace. (Romans 5:17)
- The gift of God is *eternal life*. (Romans 6:23)
- The gifts and calling of God are without repentance. (Irrevocable) (Romans 11:29)
- Gifts denote extra-ordinary powers according to grace. (Romans 12:6) We do not lack any gift. (I Corinthians 1:7; I Corinthians 12:4, 31; I Peter 4:10)
- A warning: (to all ministers which is all of us) "Neglect not the gift that is in thee, which was given thee…" (I Timothy 4:14) (This is written over the library at Southern Seminary.)
- "Meditate." I Timothy 4:15
- "Take heed unto thyself, and unto doctrine; continue in them: for in doing this thou shalt both save thyself, and them that hear thee." (I Timothy 4:16)
- "Stir up (fan into flame) the gift of the God that is in thee." (II Timothy 1:6)

No Lists of spiritual gifts is exhaustive, but are supplied according to the needs of the church.

Chapter IV.
The Fruits of the Spiritual Gifts

God's grace through the Holy Spirit gives every believer a "Spiritual" gift. It is an act of God. **Galatians 5:22, 23** reveal the result or "fruit" of the Spiritual gifts given by God and include: (Fruits are also noted in II Corinthians 3:17,18; Romans 15:13)

- Love
- Joy
- Peace
- Long-suffering
- Gentleness
- Goodness
- Faithfulness
- Meekness
- Temperance

The following may be added:
- Liberty (II Corinthians 3:17)
- Glory (II Corinthians 3:18)
- Hope (Romans 15:13)

One can surmise from the scriptures that there are countless fruits of the Holy Spirit in us waiting to be developed by His power within us. These are not to be confused with the actual Spiritual gifts. God does not give us these "fruits," but the Spirit gives us the power to develop them. (I have heard many presentations where these were described as Spiritual gifts. They should be described as the result of a Spiritual gift that we have received that gives us the power to develop these "fruits.") Faith is a Spiritual gift as noted in I Corinthians 12:9, but we develop it into a "fruit," which is faithfulness.

"Let your light so shine before men, that they may see your good works, and glorify your Father which is in heaven." (Matthew 5:16)

"Wherefore by their fruits ye shall know them." (Matthew 7:20)

"...for the tree is known by his fruit." (Matthew 12:33)

"Praying only in church, only attending church, making no contributions to church is like watering a tree that does not bear fruit." (Reference unknown) People like this hurt God, but Satan loves them.

"Now the God of hope fill you with all joy and peace in believing, that ye may abound in **hope**, through the power of the Holy Ghost." (Romans 15:13)

"Now the Lord is that Spirit: and where the Spirit of the Lord is, there is liberty." (II Corinthians 3:17)

The "fruits" of the Spirit are a major and necessary part of a Christian's life. If they are not present, then one is not a Christian. When a church does not grow it does not have fruit bearing Christian members. The question must be answered, "What is your gift and what is its fruit?"

A.   Other Moralists Lists Their Concepts of Virtues
        (15, pp. 124, 312, 705)
        (Note: They all seem to copy and seem to be based on scripture.)

I am not advocating these even though they all seem to have some merit. In a study like this they should be included to show that man many times makes up his own list of what he terms the best virtues. Modern man has shown he does this by dividing into hundreds of religious denominations. As we do this, any study will show we are getting further and further away from God's word; His letter to us, the Bible.

1. **Gregory the Great** (540-604 A.D.) listed seven deadly sins:
   - Pride (The source of all the others)
   - Envy
   - Anger
   - Dejection (Lowness of spirit)
   - Avarice (Greed)
   - Gluttony
   - Lust

2. **Tertullian,** (160 A.D. - His date of death is unknown.) He also listed his concept of the "seven deadly sins" as:
   - Idolatry
   - Blasphemy
   - Murder
   - Adultery
   - Fornication
   - False witness
   - Fraud

To other early Christians the worst sins were: "denial of the faith, murder, and gross sexual offenses." **(17, p. 215)**

3. **John Cassian** (360-435 A.D.), a monk of Southern Gaul led a protest against the fatalism of the Augustine (354-430 A.D.) doctrine of predestination. He also listed what he felt were the eight deadly sins:
   - Gluttony
   - Fornication
   - Avarice (Greed)
   - Anger
   - Dejection (Lowness of spirit)
   - Sloth (Laziness)
   - Vain Glory

- Pride

4. **St. Augustine** on his death bed quoted the seven penitential Psalms related to the seven deadly sins:
    - Pride (Psalm 32)
    - Wrath (Psalm 6)
    - Envy (Psalm 130)
    - Avarice (Psalm 102)
    - Gluttony (Psalm 38)
    - Sloth (Laziness) (Psalm 143)
    - Lust (Psalm 51)

5. **The Seven Virtues (Plato, Ambrose, Christians)**
    The first four are Cardinal Virtues by Plato: (Ambrose added those in parenthesis)
    - Prudence
    - Temperance
    - Fortitude (Patience)
    - Justice (Kindness, Unselfishness)

Christians add:
    - Faith
    - Hope
    - Love

6. **The Seven Corporal Works of Mercy** (These are required by the law of nature and are scriptural as noted in Matthew 25: 35-44)
    - Feed the hungry
    - Give drink to the thirsty
    - Clothe the naked
    - Shelter the homeless
    - Visit the sick
    - Visit prisoners
    - Ransom captives
    - **(Some add, bury the dead)**

7. **The Seven Spiritual Works of Mercy (Thomas Aquinas)**

- Teach the ignorant
- Counsel the doubtful
- Console the sad
- Reprove the sinner
- Forgive the offender
- Bear with the oppressive and troublesome
- Pray for all

8. **Benjamin Franklin** (1706-1790) one of America's most brilliant founders, statesman, author, scientist, printer, signer of The Declaration of Independence, The Articles of Confederation and The Constitution, and diplomat developed **thirteen virtues** that he had chose as his lifetime goals. They are very appropriate for this book and are: **(23, pp. 242, 243, 244.)**
   - Temperance: Drink not to elevation.
   - Silence: Avoid trifling conversations.
   - Order: Let all things have their places.
   - Resolution: Perform without fail what you resolve.
   - Frugality: i.e. Waste nothing
   - Industry: Lose no time; be always employed. (***Work as if you were to live 100 years; pray as if you were to die tomorrow***.)
   - Sincerity: Use no hurtful deceit; think innocently.
   - Justice: Wrong none by doing injuries.
   - Moderation: Avoid extremes; forbear resenting.
   - Cleanliness: Tolerate no uncleanliness in body.
   - Tranquility: Be not disturbed by trifles.
   - Chastity
   - Humility: (Imitate Jesus)

He had other famous sayings:
- Search others for their virtues, thy self for thy vices.
- Keep your eyes open before marriage, half shut afterwards.
- Freedom is not a gift from man, but a right from God.
- Self-denial is really the highest self-gratification.

- I never doubted the existence of God that he made the world, and governs it by His Providence.
- Good wives and good plantations are made by good husbands.
- Hope and faith may be more firmly grounded upon charity than charity upon hope and faith.
- Virtue is not secure until it has become habitual.
- The pleasures of this world are rather from God's goodness than our own merit.

His best for last:
- "Let no pleasure tempt thee, no profit allure thee, no ambition corrupt thee, no example sway thee, no persuasion move thee to do anything which thou knows to be evil; so thou shalt live jollily, for a good conscience is a **continual Christmas**."

Benjamin Franklin was not ashamed to relate his creed, which was: "I Believe in one God, the Creator of the Universe. That He governs by His Providence. That He ought to be worshipped."

Among his last words were a quote from Simeon (Luke 2: 29, 30), "Now lettest thou servant depart in peace, For mine eyes have seen thy salvation."

9. **The Seven Sages of Greece** (6th Century B.C.) each developed their "wise" sayings: **(21, p. 73)**
   - Know thyself
   - Nothing in excess
   - Master anger
   - Look to the end of life
   - Avoid responsibility for others' debts
   - Dedicate your blessings to God
   - Most men are bad (A Greek characteristic philosophy)
   (The sages had many other sayings.)
10. **The Ten Levels of Love** as visualized by St. John of the Cross: (1587) **(41, Pp. 649-656)**
   The life of the world is a fleeing fruition and nature without

God conceals God, but the supernatural in man reveals Him. St. John of the Cross describes the development of the love of God as going up ten steps one at a time. (The underlined scriptures were added by this author in an attempt to help St. John make his point.)

- **First Step:** The soul is convicted. It is brought low. It loses interest in sin or all things that are not of God. The soul is like a fever. One sees their soul like it is and they begin to climb. God has not been found. "Bring my soul out of prison, that I may praise thy name: the righteous shall compass me about; for thou shalt deal bountifully with me." (Psalm 142:7)
- **Second Step:** The weak soul is forced to seek God. The soul arises to seek God who loves his soul. There is a longing for this love that begins to show in words and action. The sickness of the first step becomes strength to climb to the third step. "Who maketh his angels spirits; his ministers a flaming fire." (Psalm 104:4)
- **Third Step:** The soul is forced to action. The soul fears the Lord because in God's presence as human it feels useless. The personal wickedness is too great. The immensity of God's love is beginning to be seen. Vain glory or the condemning of others goes away. "Praise ye the Lord. I will praise the Lord with my whole heart, in the assembly of the upright, and in the congregation." (Psalm 111:1) Strength and courage gain strength to go to the fourth step.
- **Fourth Step:** The soul gains a steadfast and unwearing endurance. That act and work of love becomes as strong as death. The Holy Spirit gives the soul strength to dominant the flesh. (Sin). God comes to the rescue. "Go and cry in the ears of Jerusalem, saying, Thus saith the Lord; I remember thee, the kindness of thy youth, the love of thine espousals, when thou wentest after me in the wilderness, in a land that was not sown." (Jeremiah 2:2) Personal comfort and pleasure no longer consoles the soul. The soul cries to God to be in His service and

will rejoice in suffering for Him. This fierce desire for God beings the soul to the fifth level.

- **Fifth Step:** The soul craves for God without rest or ceasing. The soul must find the love of God or die. This strong love gives strength to go to the next level. **"<u>Keep not thou silence, O God: hold not thy peace, and be not still, O God...That men may know that thou, whose name alone is Jehovah, art the most high over all the earth.</u>"** (Psalm 83:1; 18)

- **Sixth Step:** The soul fleets swiftly towards God. There is no stopping for breath. God's love has fortified the soul to fly with the swiftness of light. "But they that wait upon the Lord shall renew their strength; they shall mount up with wings as eagles; they shall run, and not be weary; and they shall walk, and not faint." (Isaiah 40:31) The soul is not entirely purified, but is placed on the seventh step.

- **Seventh Step:** God's favor showers the soul. "Beareth all things, believeth all things, hopeth all things, endureth all things." (I Corinthians 13:7) It was this level that Moses asked God the spare His people. "Yet now, if thou wilt forgive their sin--; and if not, blot me, I pray thee, out of thy book which thou hast written." (Exodus 32:32) The soul must still guard itself with great humility or fall from the other grades. The soul is bold with God and the sheer vehemence of His love pushes it up to the eighth level and unto Him.

- **Eighth step:** The soul is pressed in God's arms where it will never be released. The soul is satisfied. Some withdrew from this step. Others as Daniel remain in it: "And he said unto me, O Daniel, a man greatly beloved, understand the words that I speak unto thee, and stand upright: for unto thee am I now sent. And when he had spoken this word unto me, I stood trembling." (Daniel 10: 11) **"<u>And he said, Go thy way, Daniel: for the words are closed up and sealed till the time of the end...But go thou thy way till the end be: for thou</u>**

shalt rest, and stand in thy lot at the end of the days." (Daniel 12:9, 13.)

- **Ninth Step:** The soul is burned by the Holy Spirit to softness and proceeds toward the state of the perfect. No man can tell of the riches of God that the soul enjoys at this level. If many books were written much would be left unsaid. **"And there are also many other things which Jesus did, the which, if they should be written every one, I suppose that even the world itself could not contain the books that should be written. Amen."** (John 21:25)

- **Tenth and Last Step:** The soul is entirely assimilated to God and leaves the flesh (physical death). The soul has been purged and is with God. "Blessed are the pure in heart: for they shall see God." (Matthew 5:8) The last step rests on God. There is no longer anything hidden from the soul. We see God as He is and are like Him. **"Beloved, now are we the sons of God, and it doth not yet appear what we shall be: but we know that, when he shall appear, we shall be like him; for we shall see him as he is."** (I John 3:2) Jesus' promise is fulfilled. "And ye now therefore have sorrow: but I will see you again, and your heart shall rejoice, and your joy no man taketh from you. And in that day ye shall ask me nothing. Verily, verily, I say unto you, Whatsoever ye shall ask the Father in my name, he will give it you." (John 16: 22,23) "And the nations of them which are saved shall walk in the light of it: and the kings of the earth do bring their glory and honour into it." (Revelation 21:24) **"And he shewed me a pure river of water of life, clear as crystal, proceeding out of the throne of God and of the Lamb…And they shall see his face; and his name shall be in their foreheads…And there shall be no night there; and they need no candle, neither light of the sun; for the Lord God giveth them light: and they shall reign for ever and ever."** (Revelation 22: 1,4,5)

For love is like fire, it ever leaps upward.

11. **Henry VIII**
   - "Some men write their virtues in water." **(5, p. 695)**
   (Try to do this and you will understand the meaning.)

B. John the Baptist preached, "Repent Ye." (Matthew 3:2) "But when he saw many of the Pharisees and Sadducees come to his baptism, he said unto them, O generation of vipers…Bring forth therefore fruits needed for repentance." (Matthew 3: 7,8) "…every tree which bringeth not forth good fruit is hewn down, and cast into the fire… He that cometh after me is mightier than I, … He shall baptize you with the Holy Spirit, and with fire." (Matthew 3: 7, 8, 10, 11) (Repentance itself is not a work, but works are its inevitable fruit.)

C. Jesus said, **"Beware of false prophets, which come to you in sheep's clothing, but inwardly they are ravening wolves. Ye shall know them by their fruits… every good tree bringeth forth good fruit; but a corrupt tree bringeth forth evil fruit. A good tree cannot bring forth evil fruit; neither can a corrupt tree bring forth good fruit. Every tree that bringeth not forth good fruit is hewn down, and cast into the fire. Wherefore by their fruits ye shall know them."** (Matthew 7: 15-20.) Jesus continues with a famous and pointed statement. **"Not every one that saith unto me, Lord, Lord, shall enter into the kingdom of heaven; but he that doeth the will of my Father…Many will say to me in that day, Lord, Lord, have we not prophesied in thy name? and in thy name have cast out devils? and in thy name done many wonderful works? And then will I profess unto them, I never knew you: depart from me, ye that work iniquity."** (Matthew 7: 21-23.)

D. The question that is demanded that one must ask themselves, "What is my Gift?" (Remember every Christian has at least one.) And the second question that must be answered is, "What is the fruit or fruits of my gift or gifts?"

E. The faith *that says, but does not do* is scripturally terrible and denotes unbelief (dead). Works do not produce salvation; but true faith will always produce the fruit of good works. Those that "prophesied

133

and did wonders" did plenty of works and their confidence was in works. No one without true faith can produce true good works. (A bad tree cannot bear good fruit.)

James clearly repeats this. "But be ye doers of the word, and **not hearers only**, deceiving your own selves." (James 1:22) The word "deceiving" here is a mathematical term (reasoning alongside the facts) and refers to a miscalculation. People who call themselves Christians and are **content with only hearing the truth** without understanding have made a serious spiritual miscalculation.

F. The Law (Torah means instruction or direction)

Psalm 19: 7-9 gives 6 words, 6 evaluations, and 6 results of the Law:

Six words for the Law of God
- **Law**
- **Testimony**
- **Statutes**
- **Commandments**
- **Fear**
- **Judgments**

Six Evaluations of the Law
- **Perfect**
- **Sure**
- **Right**
- **Pure**
- **Clean**
- **True**

Six Results
- **Converting the Soul**
- **Making wise the simple**
- **Rejoicing the heart**
- **Enduring forever**

- **Righteous altogether**

This provides the key to wisdom, joy, and eternal life.

Conclusion:

Now we should be ready to hear about our spiritual gifts revealed to us by the Holy Spirit. The Holy Spirit reveals to us our free spiritual gifts, not the preacher or teacher. They do prepare us, but only if they are prepared. For these gifts we must prepare ourselves.

What is your Gift?
What is your Fruit?
One is never too old to produce the fruits of their spiritual gifts.
One is never too disabled if they are conscious to produce the fruits of their spiritual gifts.

Archeological Society

A young couple's burial site was unearthed during construction work for a factory on the outskirts of Mantua, Italy, about 25 miles south of Verona, scene of Shakespeare's "Romeo and Juliet." The remains and artifacts buried with them will be studied.

(Nation World, **The Tampa Tribune**, February 8, 2007, page 8.)
The couple was buried embraced facing each other.

What kind of love is this, 5000 years ago?

Read On!

Chapter V.
God's Love

(All true love is from God.)

In my studies of life and theology I have made what I think is a startling discovery. That is: "Many people go through life and never experience love." One is not born with love. It must be discovered, developed or revealed to one in one way or the other. Sometimes this never happens. I have observed many lives that never experienced love. The most profound examples in religious history is that of the leaders of the Inquisition and Calvin.

After reading my first non-medical book *"Mysteries of the Southern Baptist Beliefs Revealed, More Properly Called Biblical Baptist,"* and the section on divorce an old friend called me with the following story. This story also reveals that one is not born with hate. Hate must also be discovered, developed or revealed to one. He described having two wives. One taught him the meaning of hate and the other taught him the meaning of love. Then he made another profound statement, "Hate never developed in my life. It is not a part of my character. I still do not understand it. Love however, has literally invaded and taken control of my life. This did not develop until I became a true Christian."

The abbreviated story goes like this: (Keep in mind that the truths of his story came to him only in retrospect.) He married the first time at a young age. Love was not present. He simply felt that it was something that it was time for him to do. In retrospect he thinks his first wife had the same mentality. Love was not present for either of them, but the thought process computed that this was just the way marriage was supposed to be. A divorce was forced on him and it was a long time before he understood why. His conclusion was that since love was not present, there was room for hate and it developed. Evidence of this hate was revealed to him for many years.

He was lonely, alone, dazed, and confused about the major change in his life brought on by divorce. He found another person who turned all this into joy. They were married and after several years his second wife taught him the meaning of love.

I asked him if he had any real message that I could include in a future book. He said, "No, but I have friends who obviously do not have love or understand love, and some have obviously developed hate." I asked him another question, "Do you think it is possible to love and not know God?" He replied, "No! God is Love."

My perception is that most people including those who are highly educated never know "love."

In the following pages let us learn about love. When love explodes in one's life hate, if present, disappears. With God's love in one's life there is no room or place for hate. When hate is present God's love is not there. " By their fruits ye should know them."

Iris Murdoch, 1919-1999) "All of our failures are ultimately failures in love."

The entire Bible is about God's love. God's unconditional love for us was exquisitely revealed when He sent His Son to die on the cross for us. (John 3:16; I John 4:10)

Love is an attribute and nature of God. "God is love." (I John 4: 8, 16)

In our study of God's love we learn that it is beyond our ability to understand. "And to know the love of Christ, which **passeth**

knowledge, that ye might be filled with all the fulness of God."
(Ephesians 3:19)

Three stories about God's love that most people will never be able to understand:

1. A Christian physician friend called me about seeing a patient he was concerned about who had had a head injury. When I saw her she looked far beyond her years in age. You could tell that she had been quite attractive at one time. She had been "beaten-up" by her husband six or seven times according to her physician. The last time she was knocked unconscious, which was the reason for her referral to me. Her neurological exam and EEG (Brain wave) were normal. She had no permanent physical injury. I asked her why she did not leave her husband? I will remember her face and what she said all of my days. She answered, "Doctor, I just love him so much!" I did not in any way understand it at that time, but as I have gotten older and more mature with the Lord perhaps I can understand it, at least slightly. I have related this case to many people. The response has always been, "Leave the bum and have him put in jail!"

2. A remarkable story about hate being turned to love by prayer. In the 6th century a woman developed a hatred for her husband. She was willing to do everything domestic, but not live with him. She could not go to a convent since she was married. She went to a monk by the name of Columba who believed that the Bible taught the permanence of marriage. She, her husband, and the monk agreed to fast and pray. After this the woman said, "My heart has been changed from hate to love." From that day on she lived lovingly and faithfully with her husband. **(34, pp. 76, 77)**

3. **Henry Ward Beecher** said, "The crucifixion of Christ

was, on the scale and in the spheres of Infinity, which we see every day on the scale of the cradle and the nursery. The Apostle Paul, with extraordinary courage went against the whole reigning intellectual forces of the world with his faith in Christ." Beecher continues. "You never know how much one loves until you know how much he is willing to endure and suffer; and it is the suffering element that measures love." **(35, pp. 2, 3, 29)**

(The fullness of God is impossible to know, but believers can experience His greatness in our lives. The fullness of Christ is noted in Ephesians 4:13 and the fullness of the Holy Spirit in 5:18)

"...the love of God is shed abroad in our hearts by the Holy Spirit which is given unto us." (Romans 5:5)"...while we were yet sinners, Christ died for us." (Romans 5:8)

Ephesians 4:13 is the key verse of Ephesians: "Till we all come in the unity of the faith, and of the knowledge of the Son of God, unto a perfect man, unto the measure of the stature of the fullness of Christ." (Ephesians 5:18 "...be filled with the Holy Spirit.")

God's love is:

Everlasting	Jeremiah 31:3
Free	Hosea 14:4
Sacrificial	John 3:16
Enduring to the end	John 13:1

God created man in His own image. (Genesis 1:26)
God created woman for man. (Genesis 2:22)
Adam and Eve sinned.

"The LORD God made coats of skins and clothed them." (Genesis 3:21)

"God of Hosts" is the name for God that intervenes on our behalf and is always with us.

The highest disclosure and most complete proof of divine love is in our redemption. (Romans 5:8; 8:32-39; I John 4:9-10)

The love, reality and power of God can only be known by the influence of the Holy Spirit. (Romans 5:5)

The only word in the Bible translated "charity" means love.

Luther says love is "the shortest and longest divinity."

It is active. It must bless others.

Christian love is devoutness.

All human duty is summed up in love. (Matthew 22:37-40; Romans 13:8; I Corinthians 13:13)

Love is the composite of all the fruits of the Spirit. (Galatians 5:22)

Love is the number one virtue, No love, No Christian; it is the chief test. Love is the highest of all motives. Holy living is always filled with grateful love. Love is only possible with divine grace.

Love is unselfish (selflessness), but love is more than this. Unselfish is passive. Love is active. It goes beyond ones self and benefits others.

C.S. Lewis lists four kinds of love. **(36, p. 402)**
- Agape and charity are the same in the New Testament
- Philia (Friendship)
- Eros (Sexual love)
- Storge (Family affection)

A.   Agape (Charity)

- Agape (Greek), Ahaba (Hebrew)

- Agape love is the unconditional love of God for us.
- It is the highest form of love. In agape love the good of the object of love is the best interest of the object.
- It is the greatest esteem one can give.
- It is giving the other love on ones behalf.
- It is intelligent and voluntary love.
- It will last as it has a commitment between God and man.
- It is the love Christ has for the church.
- It is the love a man should have for his wife. (Ephesians 5:25)

Agape and Phileo are used interchangeable in: (Many feel these are a stylistic variation not a clear-cut difference.)
1. John 3:35 God's love for His Son.
2. John 14:21 God's love for believers
3. John 13:23 God's love for His disciple

The Agape love is the characteristic term for the love of Christianity. It is used several ways in the Bible.

1. It is the nature of God's love toward:
   a. His beloved Son (John 17:26)
   b. Human race generally (John 3:16; Romans 5:8)
   c. Believers on the Lord Jesus Christ (John 14:21)

2. It conveys God's will about His children's attitude toward one another. It is a proof of God's love and discipleship to the world. (John 13:34-35)

3. It expresses the essential nature of God (I John 4:8) **Love can only be known by its action**. It is a gift of God's Son to us. (I John 4: 9-10) Loves perfect expression is in Jesus. It is the fruit of the Spirit in Jesus in the believer. (Galatians 5:22)

B.   Phileo (Friendship)

Phileo is a just love.

It is a love of affection or ardent affection. It is translated "kiss" by Judas in Matthew 26: 48,49; Mark 14:44,45; Luke 22:48.

(A kiss in their culture was a special act of respect and affection. There were varieties such as on the back or palm of the hand, the hem of the garment, or even on the feet. Judas chose the kiss on the cheek, which showed the closest love and affection. See how despicable this was! In Mark 14:45 Judas said, "Master, Master"; and kissed Him. It appears to have been prolonged so the crowd could all identify Jesus.)

C. Erao (Eros) (Sexual love)

Strong Passionate affection
Not in the New Testament
One time in the Old Testament in Proverbs 4:6
Desires the other for itself to satisfy itself.

Jesus seemed to describe it as lust.
Matthew 5:28
Romans 1: 27; 13:14
Galatians 5:16, 17
Ephesians 4:22
II Peter 1:4
I John 2:16
I Peter 2:11
II Timothy 2:22
Proverbs 6:25 (the word "lust " is used.)

D.   Storge (Family Affection)

Storge was listed as one of the Greek words for love in the Sunday School Quarterly for retired adults in the Winter 2006-2007 edition.

These are the references below that I found in English for *storge.* It is from a root verb in Greek *stergo* meaning "to love" the mutual love between parents and their children and also between king and his people. Very rarely is it a sexual reference.

Natural affection; usually, that of parents for their offspring.
1637 <u>BASTWICK</u> *Litany* I. 11/1 We must be louing progenitors & although they doe *ex officio* abandon and renounce, both honesty and storge at once, yet we may not. **1764** <u>T. HUTCHINSON</u> *Hist. Mass.* vi. (1765) 463 The Storgée in the parent might be observed towards their young. **1809** <u>R. CUMBERLAND</u> *John de Lancaster* I. 23 The storgee, or natural affection of my daughter-in-law towards her infant. **1835** <u>KIRBY</u> *Habits & Inst. Anim.* II. xviii. 258 But first, I must say something of that *Storge*, or instinctive affection, which is almost universally exhibited by females for their progeny. **1850** <u>THACKERAY</u> *Pendennis* I. ii, I could have..adored in her the Divine beneficence in endowing us with the maternal *storge*, which.. sanctifies the history of mankind. **1880** <u>S. COX</u> *Comm. Job* 524 The Ostrich resembles the stork; but lacks its pious, maternal *storgé*.

The New Testament occurrences of "storge" that I can find are a compound form "philostorgos" Romans 12:10..where it is translated in the KJV as affectioned...and Romans 1:31...and 2 Timothy 3:3... these two are in the negative..."astorgos"...without natural affection. I could not find *"storge"* in the New Testament as a positive love without a prefix even though that is its English meaning. It is negative in the two references as noted. (Without natural affection.) We see many examples of people without "natural affections" such as in abortions, killing and abandonment of children and babies, etc.

E.   Chesed (Hesed)

Covenant love or "steadfast love" as in:
Psalm 51:1 (RSV)
Psalm 89:1 (RSV)

Loving kindness (Jeremiah 31:3)

Hebrew Hesed (desire, ardor)

Goodness
Mercy
Grace

Ahavah – Love toward ones self or another (The word "love" comes from e hav, which means, "I will give.")
(*Fifth Seal*, B. & B. Thoene, Tyndale House Publishers, 2006, p. 252)

Everlasting love: God's love for Jeremiah 31:3

Loving-kindness

"For thy lovingkindness is before mine eyes…" (Psalm 26:3)

God's loyal love and favor toward His people. In the Old Testament the word translated "loving-kindness" refers to God's long-suffering love. (His determination to keep His promises to His chosen people in spite of their sin and rebellion. Deuteronomy 7:12; Hosea 2:15-23). This lasts when the payment of sins through the sacrificial system was no longer effective. (Deuteronomy 22:22; Psalm 51:1) (God's loving-kindness is also noted in: Psalm 63:3, 103:4; Jeremiah 31:3; 32:18.)

In the New Testament the Greek word translated as "grace" best describes the idea of God's loving-kindness. Because of this all believers should treat all people with loving-kindness or grace. (Luke 6:35) All men are created in God's image and this becomes distorted. (James 3:9) Loving-kindness is a deliberate act (Not passive) to bring the sinner back to God. (Hosea 2:14-23; Romans 2:4) **(27, p. 615)**

There is a Love-Action Triangle:

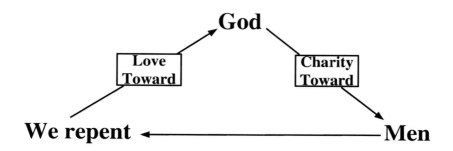

Results in
Purity toward
Oneself

Chapter VI.
Do You Love Me More Than These?

In the discussion of love in the Bible, John 21:15-25 is interesting, to say the least. It describes being specific, understanding your mission, and keeping your mind on your objective. It involves Peter. Peter's name is in the gospels more than any other except Jesus. Peter, James, and John were the "inner circle" of the twelve. Peter asked more questions than all the other apostles combined. Peter walked a short distance on water, took a coin from a fish's mouth to pay his and Jesus' taxes, denied Jesus three times, and preached at Pentecost where 3000 were saved. Jesus told him he would be martyred.

This can be considered a follow up on Matthew 26:35 where Jesus told Peter he would deny Him three times. Peter did deny Jesus three times and when the cock crowed Peter remembered and "went out and wept bitterly." (Matthew 26:75; Luke 22:62) One can imagine that Peter felt he had lost credibility with Jesus. Keep this in mind as **John 21:15-25** is reviewed.

Jesus had arisen and Peter and several of the disciples went fishing. (John 21:3) Jesus told them where to throw the nets and they became full of fish. (John 21:6) Jesus then said, **"Come and dine."** They dined on fish. (John 21:12) Jesus then precipitated His second famous discussion with Peter.

John 21:15-25:

Verse 15

Jesus said to Simon Peter, "Simon, son of Jonas, lovest thou me **more than these**?" "Lovest" here is translated for agapas as "esteem" or in kindness "more than these." (pleion touton-these persons?) The meaning of "more than these" is open to question, but can mean these "intimate friends" or even the "fish." Other suggestions include fish, boats, nets and the pleasure of fishing. (Some make a pleasure of fishing which becomes their "calling". Various occupations can "delight the senses" just as watching television or reading the newspaper, etc.

One other possible translation of "more than these" may be related to Luke 7:42 where Jesus related that the creditor who owed the most and was forgiven the most, loved the most. This could relate to a concept that one should try to excel in our love for Christ.

Peter answered, "Yea, Lord; thou knowest that I love thee." (Love here is "philo se" - love thee dearly, have ardent affection). Jesus then said, **"Feed my lambs."** (This means be an under shepherd.)

Verse 16

"He saith to him again the second time, **Simon, son of Jonas, lovest thou me?**" (Lovest here again is agapas. Note that Jesus now leaves out "more than these.") Peter answered, "Yea, Lord; thou knowest that I love thee." (Love here is philo se, love thee dearly.) Jesus said, **"Feed my sheep."**

Verse 17

Jesus said unto him the third time, **"Simon, son of Jonas, lovest thou me?"**

(Lovest is again philo-se, love me dearly, ardent affection.) Again and again Peter said surely I love thee with a high esteem and value thee with a sense of kindness, devotion, profession and repentance for my sin of three denials. Christ is putting him to the test again. In Luke 22:31, 32 Jesus said He had prayed for Simon. **"Simon, Simon, behold, Satan hath desired to have you, that he may sift you as**

wheat: But I have prayed for thee, that thy faith fail not: and when thou art converted, strengthen thy brethren." (Converted here means "converted from sin.") Peter was grieved because He said unto him the third time, **"Lovest thou me?"** Peter answered, "Lord, thou **knowest all things**; thou knowest that I love thee." Jesus said unto him, **"Feed my sheep."** Jesus is relating that He requires total devotion. This is a follow up on Jesus' words in Matthew 10:37-39, **"He that loveth father or mother more than me is not worthy of me:... he that taketh not his cross, and followeth after me, is not worthy of me. He that findeth his life shall lose it: and he that loseth his life for my sake shall find it."** (Jesus repeats that famous last sentence in Matthew 16: 24-26.)

When Jesus said, **"Feed My Lambs and My sheep."** He was being very specific. They were to be His under-shepherds. Some of His flock were lambs (young, tender, weak) and others sheep (grown, strong, and mature). The shepherd. Isaiah said, "He shall feed his flock like a shepherd: he shall gather the lambs with his arm, and carry them in his bosom, and shall gently lead those that are with young." (Isaiah 40:11) The word "feed" in verses 15 and 17 is "baske". It means give them food. The word "feed" in verse 16 is "poimaine" and is more doctrine or spiritual food.

Peter's credit in his own mind had been destroyed. When Peter said to Christ, "Thou knowest all things," he knew Christ knows his heart and that Christ had restored him to his apostleship.

The story and message to us goes on. Christ tells Peter he will suffer martyrdom. **"...but when thou shalt be old, thou shalt stretch forth thy hands, and another shall gird thee, and carry thee whither thou wouldest not."** (John 21:18) "Stretch forth thy hands," means crucifixion. He that puts on the Christ does not put off the man. The last minutes that Peter has with Christ are precious minutes.

Here is another message about how specific and firm Jesus is and how He requires absolute dedication. Peter loved John and he knew that Jesus loved John. Peter asked Jesus what would happen to John?

Jesus answered, **"If I will that he tarry till I come, what is that to thee? follow thou me."** (John 21:22)

Jesus tells him that he has too much to do and that he should not be concerned about his friend. It is none of his business. All of us, particularly military men have a sense of duty. We learn the duty is ours. The events are God's. John's future is the business of the Lord. (It is amazing that some scholars have misinterpreted this scripture to mean that John will live until Jesus comes again. It clearly says, "If I will, not that I will." John's testimony is a truth that we know from then to the present age. (John 21:24)

Chapter VII.
Summary of Epilogue

All that Christ did is not written down, but **all we need to know** is recorded. The Amen is an Amen of faith, truth, satisfaction of what is written, and **will make us wise unto salvation**. (John 21:25)

Daniel Webster (1782-1852), a Christian said, "Let our object be, our country, our whole country, and nothing but our country."

Rules From the Christian's Commander (The Trinity)

- **Be prepared**
- **Be productive**
- **Be an extension of God's love**

Remember Develop Your 3 IQ's

1. IQ (Intelligence Quotient)
As a number it's only one measure of a person's intelligence. You are born with an IQ, but you must develop basic knowledge to support it.

2. Biblical and Scriptural IQ
"Study to show thyself approved unto God..." (II Timothy 2:15) One cannot be spiritual without Biblical knowledge. "Spirituality comes about as the result of realistic Biblical discipline." (Spurgeon) If you do not understand this, you are not spiritual. Since I have been on a persistent mission to become more spiritual, I have learned

something. I am a spiritual man and a worldly man. My worldly man *does not* understand the spiritual man, but the spiritual man *does* understand the worldly man.

3. Family IQ
"Honor your father and mother." Learn "who you are" and develop yourself to the highest levels.

Do you have a Worldview?
(A Broad Mentality?)

What makes up a Worldview?
I was asked this question and initially stumbled on my own answer. Since I have given it serious thought and from my reading, travel, and experiences the following are concepts that I think are necessary for an educated worldview:

(Ones worldview will be determined by the responses to these concepts.)

1. **God**: (Accept or reject His existence.)
2. **Man or Self**: (One must know ones self to know God as He is. Is man smart enough to have an eternal opinion without a God view? Man must learn to avoid the isolated self or he will find himself a beggar, as were the old monks.)
3. **Meaning of Life**: (It's Value? Does Life have Purpose? Does each life have a specific purpose? Do you favor abortion and euthanasia?
4. **Concept of an Afterlife**: (Is anything eternal? If so, what?
5. **Truth:** (Is there an absolute truth? Is the Bible God's word or not? The number one selling book of all time cannot be ignored by any educated system. Without Bible knowledge one is illiterate regardless of the number of degrees. What is an educated person?)
6. **The World**: (Every person lives in his or her own world. How does your world relate to the real world? Are you your

"brothers keeper" or not? Does someone being murdered or starved 20,000 miles away concern you? What do you know about WAR, the Social Order, Family, the End of the World or Last Things?)

7. **Science**: (What role does science play in our lives?)

8. **The Laws and Government**: (How do you relate to the laws of your country? How do you relate to the laws of other countries? Should any person who is illiterate, (cannot read or write), has had no education, no lessons in history, knows nothing about local, state, or federal government, or does not read or speak English be allowed to vote?

9. **Religious Liberty:** (Should our educational system teach courses on the major religions? What role does ignorance play in religious liberty and what role does religious liberty play in ignorance?)

10. **What is a Worldview or Broad Mentality?** It is having an understanding of the above including: God, Man or Self, Meaning of Life, Concept of an Afterlife, Truth, The World, Science, The Laws and Government, and Religious Liberty.

Having a proper Worldview, which correlates to a Broad Mentality, determines how one regulates their lives. A person with a Broad Mentality Worldview will be able to adapt to the actual world and its oscillations. The faithful Christian does not oscillate with the world because he is the only one who has and understands absolute truth.

References:

1. *Low Back Pain, A Comprehensive Approach*, Third edition, R.M. Wolfe, D.G. Borenstein, S.M. Wiesel, Lexis Law Publishing. 2000.
2. *Malingering and Feigned Sickness*, Sir John Collie, London Edward Arnold, 1917.
3. *Breakpoint* by Charles Colson, **Florida Baptist Witness,** March 11, 2004 (Volume 121, Number 10.)
4. *"Nonorganic Physical Signs in Low Back Pain"*, Waddell G, McCullough, J.A. Kummel E, et al. **Spine** 1980; 5(2): 117-125.
5. *The Oxford Dictionary of Quotations*, Elizabeth Knowles, Oxford University Press, 2002.
6. *Bartlett's Familiar Quotations*, John Bartlett, Little, Brown and Company, 2002.
7. *The Red Badge of Courage*, Stephen Crane, The Easton Press, 1894, 1980.
8. *The Ancient Historians*, Michael Grant, Barnes and Noble Books, 1970.
9. *The Oxford History of the Classical World*, J. Boardman, J. Griffin, O. Murray, Oxford University Press, 1986.
10. *Hysteria or Pithiatism,* J. Babinski, J. Froment, University of London Press, 1918.
11. *The Treasury of the Encyclopedia Britannica*, Clifton Fadiman, Viking Penguin, 1992.
12. *"An Artifice of War"*, G.G. Liddle, **JAMA,** May 4, 1970. Vol. 212, No. 5. pp.785, 875.
13. *"Sick or Not Sick"*, **Medical World News**, April 24, 1970.
14. *"Whiplash Injuries, A Survey of 100 Cases Subsequent to Settlement of Litigation"*, Nicholas Gotten, **J.A.M.A.**, 162: 865-868.
15. *An Encyclopedia of Religion,* Vergilius Ferm, The Philosophical Library, 1945.

16. *The Oxford Dictionary of the Christian Church*, F.L. Cross and E.A. Livingstone, Oxford University Press, 1997.

17. *A History of Christianity*, K.S. Latourette, Harper and Bothers Publishers, 1953.

18. **"Welfare Overhaul Needed." The Baptist Standard**, K. Eckstrom, Religion News Service, August 4, 2006.

19. *The Ante-Nicene Fathers,* Alexander Roberts, James Donaldson, A. Cleveland Coxe, Volume II, T&T Clark Edinburgh, Wm. B. Eerdmans Publishing Co., 2001.

20. *The Ante-Nicene Fathers*, Alexander Roberts, James Donaldson, A. Cleveland Coxe, Volume III, Parts I-III, T& T Clark, Edinburgh, Wm. B. Eerdmans Publishing Co., Reprinted 1997.

21. *Brush Up Your Classics,* Michael Macrone, Gramercy Books, 1991.

22. *"Begging is Cuba's New Line of Work,"* **The Tampa Tribune**, January 1, 2007, Page 6.

23. *America's God and Country,* William J. Federer, Amerisearch, Inc. 2000.

24. *The Quotable American,* Alex Barnett, They Lyons Press, 2002.

25. *Dictionary of Quotable Definitions*, Eugene E. Brussell, Prentice-Hall, Inc., 1970.

26. *"Beggars",* **The Tampa Tribune,** January 4, 2007, Page 4.

27. *Dictionary of the Bible,* Herbert Lockyer, Sr., Thomas Nelson Publishers, 1986.

28. *"Improving the Evaluation of Permanent Impairment"*, L. Cocchiarella, M. Gurk, G. Anderson, **J.A.M.A.,** January 26, 2000, Vol. 283, No. 4, pp.532-533.

29. *"Thieves In the Temple",* **The Tampa Tribune,** January 5, 2007, pp. 1, 16.

30. *Webster's 21st Century Book of Quotations,* Thomas Nelson Publishers, 1992.

31. *The Encyclopedia of the Jewish Religion*, R.J. Zwi Werblowsky, Geoffrey Wigoder, Holt, Rhinehart and

Winston, Inc. 1965.

32. *Islam,* Ismail R. Al Faruqi, Argus Communications, 1979.
33. *Unveiling Islam*, Ergum Mehmet Caner, Emir Fethi Caner, Kregel Publications, 2002.
34. *History of the Church*, D. Jeffrey Bingham, InterVarsity Press, 1973-2002.
35. *Royal Truths*, Henry Ward Beecher, Ticknor and Fields, 1886.
36. *The Quotable Lewis,* W. Martindale, J. Root, Tyndale House Publishers, Inc., 1990.
37. *War,* Gaston Bouthoul, Walker and Company, 1953 and translated to English in 1962.
38. *"Chronic 'Takers' Disillusion Best Charity Prevails,"* Joseph Brown, **The Tamps Tribune,** November 26, 2006, p. 1.
39. *Plato, the Republic (1513),* Benjamin Jowett, The Easton Press, 1944.
40. *Wellsprings of Faith, The Imitation of Christ,* Thomas A. Kempis, (1583), Barnes and Noble, 2005.
41. *Wellsprings of Faith, The Dark Night of the Soul,* St. John of the Cross, (1587-This translation, 1900), Barnes and Noble, 2005.
42. *Greek Literature in Transition,* W. Jennings Oates, Charles T. Murphy, David McKay Company, Inc. 1944.
43. *Cyprian, His Life. His Times, His work,* Edward White Benson, MacMillina and Co., 1897.
44. *The Bible Knowledge Commentary*, John Walvoord, Ray Zuck, Cook Communications Ministries, 1983, 2000. Pp.891-893.
45. *The Septuagint With Apocryphia: Greek and English*, Sir Lancelat C. L. Brenton, Hendrickson Publishers, 1851-2001, Pp. 781-782.
46. *The Literature of the Old Testament*, Julius A. Brewer, Columbia University Press. 1922-1963. Pp 402,403.
47. *Old Testament Survey,* Charles Dyer, Eugene Merrill, Thomas Nelson Publishers, 2001, pp. 473,474.

48. *Hard Sayings of the Bible*, W.C. Kaiser, Jr., P.H. Davids, F.F. Bruce, M.T. Brauch, InterVarsity Press, 1996, Pp. 282,283.

49. *The McArthur Bible Commentary*, John McArthur, Nelson Reference and Electronic, 2005, p. 690.

50. *The Oxford Bible Commentary,* J. Barton, J. Muddiman, Oxford University Press, 2001, p. 402.

51. *The Living Word of the Old Testament*, Bernhard W. Anderson, Longman House, 1957-1988, Pp. 541-567.

52. *Matthew Henry's Commentary on the Whole Bible*, Hendrickson Publishers, 2002, Pp. 941-943.

53. *Every Name of God in the Bible*, Larry Richards, Thomas Nelson Publishers, 2001, Pp. 18,19, 21, 26, 27.

54. *The Voice, Biblical and Theological Resources for Growing Christians, Psalm 139:16 and Predestination,* Dennis Bratcher, crivoice.org/psa 139. html. 19 July 2006.

55. *The Treasury of David,* C.H. Spurgeon, Volume II, Pp. 258-292. (Not dated)

56. *The Tampa Tribune,* The Associated Press, February 23, 2007, p.16.

Printed in the United States
84904LV00004B/190-228/A